PRAISE FOR *INVEST YOURSELF*

"Millions of Catholics think they have to live a divided life, with their careers quarantined from their faith. John Abbate writes from his own hard-won experience as a businessman who not only wanted to enrich his Catholic life, but also integrate it into his business vocation. With a deft handling of business, economics, and theology, he explains clearly how you can do the same in your own work and life."

—JAY W. RICHARDS, PhD
New York Times bestselling author and host of
A Force for Good on EWTN

"This book was a journey of discovery. John Abbate brings the beauty and majesty of the Catholic faith into sharp focus, and while many of us tend to admire that beauty, this book is a call to action: to live our faith daily in our family, business, and social lives."

— STEVEN MICHAEL RAMIREZ
Former McDonald's owner-operator

"Whether you're the CEO of a For
is a suburban minivan, prepare to
for your life by studying and shar
John Abbate, a successful executive with a vibrant spiritual life,
candidly invites each of us to ask the big questions that sometimes
stand in the way of the true prosperity God desires for us. God
desires our best and wants to give us the best! Dare to commit
yourself to true encounter, lasting change, and the abundance that
comes from mission-oriented vision."

— LISA M. HENDEY
Author of *The Grace of Yes*

INVEST
YOURSELF

INVEST YOURSELF

DARING TO BE CATHOLIC IN TODAY'S BUSINESS WORLD

JOHN M. ABBATE

BEACON PUBLISHING
North Palm Beach, Florida

Published by Beacon Publishing

Design by Madeline Harris

ISBN: 978-1-63582-023-2 (softcover)
ISBN: 978-1-942611-87-5 (ebook)

Names: Abbate, John M., author.
Title: Invest yourself : daring to be Catholic in today's business world / John M. Abbate.
Description: North Palm Beach, Florida : Beacon Publishing, 2018.
Identifiers: LCCN 2017057174 | ISBN 9781635820232 (softcover : alk. paper) | ISBN 9781942611875 (e-book)
Subjects: LCSH: Work—Religious aspects—Catholic Church. | Vocation—Catholic Church. | Wealth—Religious aspects—Catholic Church. | Success—Religious aspects—Catholic Church.
Classification: LCC BX1795.W67 A23 2018 | DDC 248.8/8—dc23

For more information on this title or other books and CDs available through the Dynamic Catholic Book Program, please visit www.DynamicCatholic.com.

The Dynamic Catholic Institute
5081 Olympic Blvd • Erlanger • Kentucky • 41018
Phone: 1-859-980-7900
Email: info@DynamicCatholic.com

First printing, January 2018

Printed in the United States of America

ACKNOWLEDGMENTS

To my wife, I am so blessed and appreciative of your influence on my faith and vocational journey these past thirty years. You are the perfect antidote to my personality, and you have impacted my life beyond measure. Thank you for the support and courage that allowed me to tell a bit of our story. Your love, empathy, and self-giving are truly unmatched.

To my mom, a huge thanks and gratitude for your faith, encouragement, and dedication to our entire extended family. I am indebted to your love and commitment to raising a Catholic family.

To my dad, you are the epitome of reverent leadership. What an incredible role model you have been for me and others.

To Our Lady Queen of Peace for her unrelenting call that first led me on a pilgrimage to Medjugorje, and the never-ceasing challenge to live a life uncommon.

To my children, Matthew, Kathryn, and Andrew, what a gift from God you three are to your mom and me. I strive each and every day to be the kind of father to you that my dad is to me . . . though your Poppy is a tough act to follow. Let us strive to keep the legacy alive.

To Monsignor Joseph Pacheco for his early encouragement and unwavering belief in my talents and abilities.

To my brothers and sister, we have always challenged each other to keep our faith at the center of our lives. You are the source of much of my joy and inspiration.

To my brother Jim and friends Brian, Steve, Jamie, and Doug, your guidance, perspective, and example have been invaluable to me as a husband, father, and friend.

To Katherine Adams for your early help in challenging me to focus my message and guidance in the editing of the raw manuscript.

To the leadership at Dynamic Catholic for their vision, courage, and belief in the power of the laity to lift the Catholic Church in American to a new level of passion and purpose.

Lastly, to the team at Beacon Publishing for their fresh insight and advice on creating a manuscript that ultimately reflects my intended idea and mission.

CONTENTS

ONE

Choosing Prosperity

We make a living by what we get.
We make a life by what we give.
—Winston Churchill

The most extraordinary power we have been given as human beings is our freedom to choose. St. Thomas Aquinas eloquently called it "the dignity of causality."[1] Simply stated, this means that through the power of our free will and intellect given to us by God, we have the capacity to decide the direction of our own life and our own prosperity. We can choose whether to make a lasting difference that sees beyond a temporal world bound by scarcity and fear or simply toil through life seeking perpetual self-gratification, never reaching true fulfillment.

I believe most of us would agree that we all want three basic things out of our brief time here on earth. We all need hope; we all yearn for happiness; and we all crave the satisfaction of knowing that our life has counted for something. These three elements constitute a life well lived—an abundant life.

But living such an abundant life requires tapping into our essential purpose as human beings—a purpose that is far greater than realizing the fulfillment of our own desires or passions.

Because we are created in the image and likeness of God (see Genesis 1:27), we can start by looking at him. And there we discover that the essence of our authentic humanity is in self-giving. This is our Christian inheritance, powerfully expressed by Christ and his teachings. Self-giving is the key that will free us from the burdens of a world dominated by the "scarcity mentality" we have inherited.

We all have the potential to live a life of Christian abundance now, regardless of the reality of our past choices. Yet this is possible only when we deliberately and courageously decide to think differently about our life's vocation and are willing to exercise choices to live this higher calling. In this book, using my own journey as the backdrop, I will explore the concept of vocation as the medium to live out our God-given purpose, live a life that matters, and experience the true abundance we desire.

I am a very practical and logical thinker, and most of my life has been dominated by the norms of the business world. Deep down, I am a finance and economics guy. I love creating a good spreadsheet and analyzing the next opportunity. I truly enjoy the everyday challenge and unpredictability of maintaining financial, personal, and professional success.

Along the meandering path of my life, I have discovered a few things about how to balance my financial portfolio, and more crucially, my personal and faith lives as well. Of course, I still fail at times, yet the risk of catastrophic failure is mitigated when I am living my true vocation.

My Catholic faith is not an exercise in irrationality or credulity. It is a faith built first and foremost on God and the revelation of his son, Jesus, but also centered on the wisdom and intellect of thousands of men and women who have come before me. Most of these men and women have spent their entire lives dedicated to the rigorous scholarship of this discipline called theology. Catholicism is steeped in the rationality, wisdom, and practicality of being scrutinized, studied, and applied in our culture for two thousand years. Isn't it time we stopped believing that our Catholic faith is built on foolish and nonsensical imagination or arcane mysticism? As you read this book, I will introduce you to a few of the brilliant thinkers who have dedicated themselves to Christ and worked selflessly to make these truths accessible to the rest of us.

I hope that as I share my own journey and discoveries, you will gain a deeper understanding of the fact that business success and a thriving Catholic faith aren't mutually exclusive, but instead together can form the basis of a life of abundance—a life that is rich in what matters to God.

I've learned how investing in both the practical and spiritual matters of life have revolutionized the way I live, and I hope to share these ideas with you in a way that is engaging, entertaining, educational, and practical. I believe that the hope, happiness, and meaning we all seek can only be found in Jesus Christ and a life of self-giving rather than self-serving. This is the foundational message of this book, and it sums up our vocational call as Christians.

Standing on the Shoulders of Giants

I have had a lifelong passion for biographies. I love the unique and inspiring stories I've encountered through reading about the lives and accomplishments of others. When we hear or read about the ways another person overcomes adversity or lives with excellence, it allows us to think and relate differently to our own lives and our not-so-unique struggles. As Sir Isaac Newton put it, "If I have seen further, it is by standing on the shoulders of giants."

Immersing myself in stories about Jack Welch, Ronald Reagan, Immaculée Ilibagiza, Thomas Merton, John Adams, Albert Einstein, St. John Paul II, Steve Jobs, St. Francis of Assisi, St. Catherine of Siena, and Jesus Christ has allowed me to find common ground with their lives, their struggles, and their successes and failures. Their candid self-revelation and vulnerability have led me to reexamine my own reality and allow a deeper examination of my core ideology.

I cannot overstate the power these stories and others have had on my life and my evolution as a businessman, father, husband, and struggling Catholic. Much of my reading in my late teens and early adulthood was focused on business and politics. Over the past twenty years, I've developed an insatiable appetite for reading the profiles of successful businesspeople in books and in magazines such as *Businessweek* and *Forbes*. I have been driven by a desire to unlock the mystery of other people's success and gain insight into their motivation.

I thought that understanding the success drivers of these men and women would propel me to maximize my own potential. However, once I saw beyond the secular world's view of success, I became disenchanted with much of the material provided by many of these books and magazines.

Through years of personal and professional growth and failure, I have defined my own principles, vision of success, and process for attainment. I no longer need to spend my time reading others' stories of business success or failure. One more story of a person working seventy hours a week and making a financial windfall has become stale and uninspiring.

My experiences with Catholic conferences, pilgrimages, and professional business organizations such as Legatus have opened my eyes to the abundance of talented and faithful men and women who are willing and able to carry on the mission of the Church. These heroic people are the future of this great faith. Their enthusiasm, sacrifice, and talent are infectious.

Unfortunately, the vast majority of Catholics never see much of the charismatic and inspirational side of our Church. Many don't seek out opportunities to hear great Catholic speakers, experience Mass in new and inspiring locations, spend a week on pilgrimage with other Spirit-filled Catholics, or read a great book about these dynamic members of our faith.

Instead, they are bombarded with stories told through the lens of the secular and slanted media of fallen priests and fringe groups whose idea of pro-life work is bombing women's clinics.

The stories of individual Catholics that the media reports are equally unfortunate. They are not the stories of ordinary Catholics doing extraordinary work in their communities. Media reports focus on marginal Catholic celebrities or politicians who do not embody the faith and the teaching of the Church. They use their celebrity status to promulgate their distorted and individualistic versions of the truth.

Disappointingly, statistics say that less than 1 percent of Catholics will read a single Catholic book in the course of a year. The true beauty of the Catholic faith can be fully realized only when we utilize our intellect to acquire knowledge to grow in our faith. We aren't meant to have a blind and uninformed spiritual journey. Our faith takes real effort and scholarship.

In the encyclical *Fides et Ratio* (*Faith and Reason*), St. John Paul II reiterates the natural inclination we have to seek truth using our innate creative intelligence: "We ultimately seek the truth because 'in the far reaches of the human heart there is a seed of desire and nostalgia for God.' God has created man with an internal homing device so that we may long to seek his truth and peace" (24).

We simply cannot divorce faith from reason if we are to truly understand our relationship with God and his purpose for our life. It is reason that sheds the light that allows our faith to prosper. Without a proper philosophical understanding of God, faith becomes merely a blind and childish trust that can be easily manipulated by other people. However, without faith, pure rationalism and scientific positivism will also lead man down a path of carnage. A simple look at the history of the past century proves what happens when man relies predominantly on his rational nature for guidance. In hindsight, we can all agree that there was nothing remotely rational about the leadership and subsequent genocide inflicted by people such as Hitler, Mao, and Stalin. Yet all three of these men had one thing in common: a belief in the power of the secular over the divine.

Jesus' death on the cross is a stark revelation that God's saving plan is not congruent with human logic. "God chose what is foolish in the world to shame the wise . . . God chose what is low and despised in the world, things that are not, to reduce to nothing things that are" (1 Corinthians 1:27–28).

Therefore, the wisdom of God cannot be fully understood or contained by human reasoning. Only through revelation and faith can we come to fully know and understand God's salvific plan for us.

In *Fides et Ratio*, John Paul II writes that through the paschal mystery—Jesus' life, death, and resurrection—we are given the opportunity via faith to get a glimpse of our Father's plan for us. Therefore, Christ is the link between philosophy and faith that allows us to overcome our human limitations.[2]

Millions of Catholic Books

Books can change lives. Books allow us to see beyond the limited walls of our daily existence and share our insight and wisdom with each other. As C. S. Lewis said, "We read to know we are not alone."[3]

I've discovered that most Catholics want to understand their faith on a deeper level, but not necessarily via traditional Catholic channels provided through their parish. They want to be inspired in their faith through heartwarming or interesting stories that can translate to their own life. Most Catholics are not interested in reading about the theology of consubstantiation, transubstantiation, or in-depth Christology. People want to spend their valuable and limited time on topics that directly relate to their lives today. They'd like to know how this book can help them on their unique path to becoming better, happier, more hopeful people. And readers are looking for material that not only teaches and entertains but also inspires them to action.

The mystery for us fragile and broken humans is to understand what motivates people of talent to push themselves in a direction that is so countercultural. This gap in understanding has the potential to compel and captivate us to seek not only answers for their life's path, but ultimately the answers for our life's path.

Based on my own experience, it is a joy to appreciate firsthand the power and mystery of our faith, and share it with other dedicated and inspired Catholics. Our Church is rich in tradition and talent; however, we must be willing to explore and seek the opportunities that are available to us. This cannot happen when we confine our faith journey to a single parish or attending Mass once per week.

However, books can only point the way to a new faith in Christ. As Pope Francis wrote in an encyclical letter to the bishops, "Faith is born of an encounter with the living God."[4] We encounter him in the sacraments, through reading and meditating on Scripture, and in experiencing a vital, ongoing relationship with Jesus Christ in prayer. Encountering the living God in these ways empowers us to live fully and deeply, enjoying the abundance we long for and that God has planned for us since the beginning.

The Challenge of Sharing Our Faith in Today's Culture

To speak or write publicly about my Catholic faith journey and the ways in which I strive to integrate it in my life, work, family, and culture is always a challenge for me. It is much easier to talk about topics such as finance, marketing, and entrepreneurship, which relate to my business. These are the things I know so well; they are much less personal, and allow for much less vulnerability. When it comes to sharing my faith, I am forced to face the reality of my fragile humanity. And so are you.

We are all acutely aware of our unique shortcomings, and no one wants to feel like a hypocrite. That's why many times we remain silent. We dismiss our role in the mission of sharing our faith and hope with others rather than accept our past shortcomings. It reminds me of the following story in the Gospel of Mark.

Jesus is in a synagogue in the town of Capernaum. It is very early in his ministry. Already he is an enigma; certainly he's not well known or understood by the people around him. In this synagogue, Jesus meets a man with an unclean spirit that immediately confronts him.

The demonic spirit that has possessed this man is the only one who truly recognizes Jesus for who he is: the Son of God. The spirit basically says to Jesus in a harsh, angry voice: "I know who you are, Jesus of Nazareth! What do you want with me?"

"I know who you are!" Those are the troubling words that run through our minds as we think about our life's purpose, the mission God has for us. Those words play on our insecurities, our history, our fears. This is what confronts us when we have an opportunity to share our faith with someone; it's a false voice that claims to know who we are and what we have done in betrayal of our faith. This voice wants to shut us down, keep us from being true to our mission, and shame us with the actions of our past, creating just enough doubt and discomfort to silence us.

But while we must embrace the reality of our failings and imperfections, it is still true that God uses us to reach each other for the kingdom. Thomas Merton said, "It is Christ who draws us to himself through the action of our fellow men."[5] So, to speak about one's faith journey is the way Christ reaches others, even though it demands a certain amount of acceptance, vulnerability, and most of all, humility.

St. Paul said this in Romans 7:21–25:

> So I find it to be a law that when I want to do right, evil lies
> close at hand. For I delight in the law of God, in my inmost
> self, but I see in my members another law at war with the law
> of my mind and making me captive to the law of sin which
> dwells in my members. Wretched man that I am! Who will de-

liver me from this body of death? Thanks be to God through Jesus Christ our Lord!

I find this to be an incredibly poignant passage from St. Paul. I can certainly relate to his struggles and frustrations when I reflect on my own life experiences. I am constantly fighting attitudes and behaviors that I know are contrary to God's desire for me as well as to my true desires. I fall victim again and again to the fragile humanity of a will affected by sin. However, I am consoled by St Paul's message of liberation through the resurrection of Jesus Christ and his living Church.

I have come to understand that it is the future that tells us what our past is about. It is our life experience that allows us to become that unique self-gift that we are called to be for others. The most compelling form of evangelization comes when people are willing to share their personal encounter with Christ. As humans, we connect with stories. They move us, draw us in, and captivate our attention. I believe we must push ourselves outside our comfort zone and into our past in order to draw on the experiences that allow us to pave the way for others.

We keep our heritage alive by telling our unique stories, keeping our traditions, cooking our cultural foods, and finding time to be together as a family. It is our history and our connection to our past. The power of our Catholic culture is built upon our faith tradition. We partake of the sacraments, celebrate feast days, and learn from the teachings of the Church. We must dare to share our story with those around us and invite others to tell their stories as well.

We have all received an abundant inheritance from our forefathers. We stand on the shoulders of so many resilient and courageous figures of our past. Today *we* must choose to be the link that keeps our Catholic history alive in our families, our communities, and our culture. When we choose to learn about and share our own family history and embrace the richness of the tradition of our Catholic faith, we become the instrument that continues the mission of Matthew 28. We spread the Good News to all corners of the world.

Passing on the Legacy

When I was a teenager, my brothers and I would spend time in the late evenings with my father just hanging out in our spa. We would talk about his early childhood, college life, his work, and the Catholic faith. He would tell us stories of his upbringing during the Great Depression, and the struggles and joys of a childhood during this period of America's history. He would also talk about his family's daily commitment to its Catholic faith and why he had held so steadfastly to it throughout his life. Whether it was the fear and guilt of missing Mass on a Sunday, an obligation to eat fish on Fridays all year long, or always seeking a Catholic Church to say a prayer in when he first moved to a new town, these were the stories of his faith, and through this sharing they become the stories of our faith as well.

My mother and father have always been committed Catholics. As children, missing Mass on Sundays was never an option for us. My parents have never been overly pious, but simply matter-of-fact as to how and why the Catholic faith is the best and most practical way to live your life. They have passed on the traditions of their faith to their grandchildren as well. They both place great importance on the sacraments of baptism and first Communion, and their vital importance as lifetime gifts of grace to heal and elevate the human spirit in times of triumph and tragedy. As Pope Francis says, "Do you open your hearts to the memories that your grandparents pass on? Grandparents are like the wisdom of the family; they are the wisdom of a people."[6]

I am Catholic because of these two people. They are my original connection to the beauty and majesty of this two-thousand-year-old culture. What an incredible gift it has been!

As you read this book, I hope you take the opportunity to consider your own unique life experiences, both the good and bad, in shaping your mind and heart toward a life in Christ.

TWO

In the Beginning . . . There Was Economics

The economy of salvation refers to God's activity in
creating and governing the world, particularly to his plan
for the salvation of the world in the person of Jesus Christ,
a plan which is being accomplished through His Body the
Church, in its life and sacraments.
—CCC, Glossary

As we begin our pursuit of true prosperity, it makes sense to explore the impact and implications of economics on our faith journey. I think we can agree that humans are all driven by the temporal nature of the earth and the impact of a world defined in many ways by its limited resources. The reality is that many of our daily behaviors are directed by our innate fear of this scarcity, as well as the subsequent application of the laws of supply and demand we use to manage the problem. This phenomenon is commonly referred to as our biological anthropology, and it creates the foundation for a society that is governed by the science of economics.

As Christians, we grasp that we are eternally connected with our original parents, through the consequences of original sin. Because of them, we struggle to manage the limitations imposed on our lives. And that's where God's economics enter the picture—his activity as he governs the world and plans for its salvation through Christ. The Church now carries on this grand economy of salvation.

The role of economic management has always had a deep history within the context of our evolution and our Catholic faith as well. Whether in St. Paul's letters or in parables within the Gospels, we find many direct references to the word *economics*, along with the overarching theme of managing our lives within financial parameters.

The etymology of the word *economics* is from the original Greek word *oikos*, which means "house." The *oikonomos* would describe the "steward" or "manager" of the house. The *oikonomia*, or "economy," is the plan for the management of the house. The evolution of this concept, starting with the household, has led to our current understanding of modern economics and the process of managing not only our household but also state, national, and international economies.

St. Paul was pastoral in his approach to evangelization. He was always very concerned with the implementation of our faith, with the "how" of living our faith in culture. That's why he spoke and wrote often on the topic of economics. St. Paul's intent was to help the early Christians understand how to manage their house or family (*oikos*) and larger community/economy (*oikonomia*) in light of the new and very radical philosophy of Jesus Christ.

Existing and managing ourselves within economic boundaries is a focal concern in Christianity. The challenge of daring to live the radical message of Christ in the marketplace is the preeminent struggle for all of us. We all face the reality of the necessity of work to support our biological needs and those of our families.

But what happens once we have met the basic needs for our family and ourselves? Is it acceptable to want more? How do we reconcile the fact that we are all given different gifts, but some are compensated at a much higher level than others? What is our responsibility to acknowledge this disparity, and are we called to then redistribute?

Our faith must be lived in the cultural and economic reality of a world that has provided many of us with a material abundance far beyond our basic needs. How do we deal with the complicated by-product of capitalism and stay in right relationship with God's family? How do we administer the nonessential wealth that our labor has produced?

These are just a few of the questions that I have reflected upon over the past twenty-five years. In the next several chapters, I'll share some of my struggles, and I hope it will shed some light on your path and give you a better understanding of these age-old, often troubling questions.

Basis of Economics: Scarcity

The first lesson of economics is scarcity: There is never enough of anything to fully satisfy all those who want it. The first lesson of politics is to disregard the first lesson of economics.
—*Thomas Sowell*

I was first introduced to the theory of economics in 1983. I was a senior in high school, taking the first of many economics classes. Mr. Paske, one of the few teachers I still remember from those days, was witty, with a sarcastic sense of humor. He was the perfect antidote for a bunch of smug and self-absorbed high school seniors.

Learning about macroeconomics was a profound intellectual experience for me. It all made so much sense. Mr. Paske taught me the logical principles behind how and why the world seemed to work on a financial and economic level. This introduction to the science of economics would eventually lead me to seek an undergraduate degree in economics in college. Thus, I began my journey toward seeing the world through the eyes of an economist.

Just for clarification, I am not an economist. Having an undergraduate degree in economics is the equivalent of having an undergraduate degree in psychology. I am just qualified enough to be an annoyance at Thanksgiving dinner. However, being familiar with the basic principles of economics has helped me more fully understand the actions of humanity in a world defined by limited resources.

Throughout most of human history, the overarching problem was simply surviving. The bulk of everyday life was spent seeking a share of a limited supply of food, water, shelter, warmth, and safety. As a species, humans existed on the brink of starvation and with the threat of physical harm for thousands of years. Even up to a hundred years ago, most of humanity continued to struggle with problems of scarcity.

Until the latter part of the twentieth century, most of people's waking hours were spent on work or household chores. During the mid-1800s the average man worked sixty-five to seventy hours per week with virtually no leisure time. One hundred years ago, less than 10 percent of the workforce actually took vacations.

Interestingly enough, in 1848 a famous economist named John Stuart Mill described a scenario in his book *Principles of*

Political Economy. He wrote of a future in which there would be enough economic growth for mankind. He truly felt that at some point, economic output and productivity would render a certain material contentment in society. When that time arrived, people would be able to work less or not at all, while enjoying material goods, along with the time to pursue the higher goals of life. Mill wrote:

> There would be as much scope as ever for all kinds of mental culture, and moral and social progress; as much room for improving the Art of Living, and much more likelihood of its being improved, when minds ceased to be engrossed by the art of getting on. Even the industrial arts might be as earnestly and as successfully cultivated, with this sole difference, that instead of serving no purpose but the increase of wealth, industrial improvements would produce their legitimate effect: that of abridging labour.

I find this to be an extraordinarily interesting thought to ponder from today's perspective. John Stuart Mill assumed that man had the capacity to eventually overcome the psychological and physical encumbrance of scarcity and desire. He could have never imagined the amount of goods and services provided by today's economy. But what would have baffled him even more is the insatiable appetite man still has for acquiring more stuff, and the fear of losing out on the incremental nature of having more. He certainly could never have envisioned humanity waiting in line outside overnight for the opportunity to buy the latest iPhone.

The simple reality is that there is still never enough of anything to satisfy our deeply embedded materialistic and scarcity mentality. You need look no further than our national debt statistics. Today our consumer debt is at a record high of $12.84 trillion. Our credit card debt makes up more than $784 billion of the total, with the average monthly unpaid credit card balance at $16,883 per household.[7] What happened to the so-called "new normal" postrecession mentality that was so highly discussed in the years following the 2008–2009 recession?

The late philosopher George Santayana wrote, "Those who cannot remember the past are condemned to repeat it." Based on the current evidence, it seems a decade is just about enough time to forget the post-austerity mentality of the most recent recession.

Certainly the philosophies of individualism and materialism can be directly linked with our deeply embedded biological anthropology: greed, envy, and fear of scarcity. Obviously, Mill underestimated the instinctive nature of their power and grip on humanity as a whole.

As we have started to overcome the physical struggles of the true scarcity faced by our ancestors, we are still psychologically burdened with their legacy. We are innately fearful of not having enough for our family and ourselves. Yet the most fundamental embodiment of scarcity that impacts our lives is time. The late economist Gary Becker pointed out that even in a utopian world where price and quantity reach an equilibrium that mitigates the fear of material deficiency, we must deal with the issue of scarcity of time. Regardless of one's accumulation of wealth, the reality of the physical flow of time still provides us only a finite period to consume and purchase.

The Greek word for *time* is *chrónos*, which refers to the unending chronology of the physical nature of the earth moving around the sun; this is the passage of physical time. It is this unending cycle of movement that creates an ever-widening gap from our past, as well as the perpetual aging of our bodies. *Chrónos* embodies the scarcity of time that causes the anxiety of facing (literally and metaphorically) the reality of aging and lamenting life's missed opportunities.

However, the Greeks had another word for time, *kairos*, which can be found in the New Testament. This implication of time suggests a transcendence of the constraints of a physical time subject to scarcity. Whereas *chrónos* is quantitative (seconds and minutes), *kairos* is qualitative, measuring moments, not seconds. It refers to the meaningful moment, the perfect moment, the next significant moment.

In Ephesians 5, St. Paul instructs us to redeem the *kairos*, meaning to pay attention and take advantage of the opportune times and seasons of our lives. It is a perspective that sees life not as seconds, minutes, or hours slipping through our fingers like sand, but as unique moments of opportunity to live our faith in culture. If we are physically and psychologically bound by the constraints of our temporal world, the element of time will always be a limited resource for us, and a major cause of anxiety.

Fear of Scarcity

You can never have enough of what you don't really need.
—Matthew Kelly

As humans we all must come face-to-face with the economic reality of limited resources and the impact of supply and demand in our life. Scarcity and competition have led humans down a very slippery slope, a path where we begin to act and react out of the fear that they kindle within our psyche. It is a fear that grips us and leads us to irrational thought and actions. It leads to feelings of panic and anxiety, which results in poor choices: corruption, deceit, violence, or some other form of sin that distances us from God and each other. Make no mistake—sin is often foundationally rooted in fear. Perhaps that's why St. John Paul II started his entire papacy with a simple but profound statement: "Be not afraid."

The reality is that we all must deal with our natural fear of scarcity; it grips us all. This is a by-product of our history; it's our innate desire to survive. It's our biological anthropology. We need look no further than any history book, including the Bible, for confirmation of our capacity to allow scarcity and fear to dictate irrational behavior that has led to much murder, deceit, and sin. The twentieth century turned out to be the bloodiest period in history. Unfortunately, the twenty-first century is continuing along this same path of annihilation. As Thomas Merton wrote, "The world is the unquiet city of those who live for themselves and are therefore divided against one another in a struggle that cannot end, for it will go on eternally in hell."[8]

All of us have acted irrationally due to our natural inclination toward these fears. Take a moment and examine your own life. How have you acted when faced with the fear of missing out on some material good? Can you remember a time when fear and greed led you down a path toward excessive risk against your better judgment? How did you react to the housing bubble of the early 2000s, and the subsequent crash? How did the stock market drops of 2000 and 2008 affect you?

Take some time to examine other areas of your life that have been influenced by feelings of scarcity and fear. Maybe those areas were financially related, or maybe they were influenced by your self-esteem. Here are some examples:

- The desire for that critical job promotion
- The "perfect" girlfriend or boyfriend who led you down a path of sin
- The perfect house that you just had to have, so you overextended yourself
- The scarcity and panic of missing out on the bull market. Everyone was getting rich but you, so you bought at the top and eventually sold at the bottom, like 85 percent of investors.
- The need to get your "brilliant" child into that elite college
- The simple daily battles in life, such as fighting for your seat at the airport, fighting traffic on the way to work, or fighting to get your money's worth at Disneyland

There is no denying that we all must find a way to deal with the reality of our innate fear of losing and that overwhelming desire to be the first in a world of limited supply.

The *Catechism of the Catholic Church* and theologians in general have spent a considerable amount of time reflecting on the issues we face. In fact, one of Catholicism's pivotal concepts in dealing with scarcity is the belief in the transcendental nature of faith and its impact on the constraint of time, or *chrónos*. The Church believes that we are nothing more than sojourners on this earth, pilgrims on the path to heaven.

Through Christ's life, death, and resurrection, he has not only conquered death—he has conquered time. No longer do we need to be bound by a limited life that ends in death. We can truly see our time on earth as a bridge to greater possibilities. We can learn to see time in a fresh, new context.

How would you spend your life differently if you truly embraced the idea of a lifetime of abundance rather than scarcity? Would you take more opportunity to savor the beauty of God's natural creation, choose to delve into a more satisfying vocation, or simply invest in deeper relationships? The emotional and physical toll of living with time as a limited resource certainly shapes our worldview and, sadly, our actions.

With that understanding, let's delve into the "theology" of American capitalism.

American Capitalism and Our Catholic Faith

American capitalism has been the philosophical and practical antidote to counterbalance the challenges related to the earth's limited resources. I am certainly a part of this culture and have been rewarded for my ability to maximize the opportunities afforded by the system of commerce. I do believe capitalism is the most efficient way we have to allocate the earth's limited resources and to redistribute wealth.

America was the very first country built on an economic foundation based on individual responsibility and the freedom of initiative. The United States has been the safe haven for the world's entrepreneurs, small business owners, and the poor seeking the opportunity to maximize their talents and expand their dreams. This was the foundation our forefathers envisioned and the inspiration for the industrial revolution of Europe.

Today we live in the wealthiest country in the history of the world. The per capita material abundance of the United States is truly astonishing by any measure. However, that does not mean we don't have issues with uneven distribution of wealth or pockets of abject poverty in America. Yet the reality is that even the "poor" in this country would be considered very well off in much of the world. As of 2015, according to the United States Department of Health and Human Services, a family of four in the United States is considered poor if their household income falls below $24,250.

According to Gallup research, the median household income in the United States is $43,585. As a comparison, again based on research done by Gallup, the worldwide median household income is just under $10,000 per year, with most of Africa, Asia, Mexico, South America, and Eastern Europe averaging far below this number.[9] According to that data, capitalism has tremendous power to elevate the wealth of a society, but it is only a tool of the people, and thus dependent on their execution and intentions.

Today, the philosophical tradition of entrepreneurship and capitalism is on trial. There is much dissension and debate over disparity of income, class distinction, and the role and responsibility of government in our lives. As of 2016, the United States has some of the highest tax rates in the world on individuals and corporations. The debates continue to rage as to the "right" form of governmental intervention in the economic system of our society.

I believe it is important that we understand what the wisdom of our faith has to tell us on these contentious issues pertaining to capitalism and wealth distribution. If you're not familiar with it, you might be surprised at the Church's position in this debate. St. John Paul II addressed Catholic social teaching with regard to capitalism:

> If by "capitalism" it is meant an economic system which recognizes the fundamental and positive role of business, the market,

private property and the resulting responsibility of the means
of production, as well as free human creativity in the economic
sector, then the answer is certainly affirmative, even though
it would perhaps be more appropriate to speak of a "business
economy," "market economy," or simply a "free economy."[10]

However, he goes on to remind us that capitalism must be
"circumscribed within a strong juridicial framework which places it at the service of human freedom in its totality."[11]

The words of Pope John Paul II certainly support the notion
of capitalism, but with several caveats to consider. The key elements that define a better understanding of capitalism on behalf
of the common good are as follows:

- a free and democratic state where people are allowed to exercise their own will and intellect
- a sophisticated governmental judicial system to handle civil
  disagreement
- a culture that embodies natural moral law

The esteemed Catholic author Michael Novak built upon the
foundational benefits and justification of capitalism in *The Spirit
of Democratic Capitalism*. At one time, Novak believed in socialism
because he felt its economic system seemed ethically superior.
However, he realized through observation of human affairs and
personal reflection that he was mistaken. He grew to understand
that capitalism is superior to socialism, both in practice and in
theory. Most important, Christian virtues can not only survive,
but can flourish under democratic capitalism. In this seminal
work Novak states:

Few theologians or religious leaders understand economics, industry, manufacturing, trade and finance. Many seem trapped in pre-capitalist modes of thought . . . Many swiftly reduce all morality to the morality of distribution. They demand jobs without comprehending how jobs are created. They demand the distribution of the world's goods without insight into how the store of the world's goods may be expanded . . . They claim to be leaders without having mastered the techniques of human progress.[12]

Democratic capitalism taps an individual's God-given creativity and initiative and relies on self-interest to direct its actions. It offers an outlet for greed and reinforces habits of prudence, fortitude, and tolerance if one is to be successful in his or her endeavors. These virtues are consistent with Christianity and are reflective of the Protestant work ethic that has so profoundly influenced commerce in the early days of our country.

Modern economic thought tends to have a zero-sum concept of man, nature, and wealth. This view implies that no gain can be realized without a subsequent cost. No one can obtain material wealth without it being taken from someone else. It follows that without strong control by government, there would be perpetual conflict and each person would seek to maximize his or her own gain. Thus, control is needed to prevent excessive individualism and avarice. Under the socialist view, capitalists become wealthy by exploiting workers, and nations become wealthy by exploiting Third World nations. Of course, the ultimate solution to end such abuse is the elimination of private property.

Much of Catholic social teaching was formed in the precapitalist world of medieval society, which appreciated stability rather than dynamic economic growth. The Church teachings were thus more concerned with the fair distribution of available goods than with an economic system that created incremental long-term societal wealth based on exponential growth.

Certainly the New Testament supports the poor. The spirit of socialism thus initially appears to be closer to the Gospel than the competitive nature of capitalism. However, by fostering a form of capitalism that values freedom, individualism, and innovation, society as a whole is lifted to greater economic prosperity.

Today, the Catholic Church stands firm in its position on the role of democratic capitalism to enhance the mission of the Church:

> The illusion that a policy of mere redistribution of existing wealth can definitively resolve the problem must be set aside. In a modern economy, the value of assets is utterly dependent on the capacity to generate revenue in the present and the future. Wealth creation therefore becomes an inescapable duty, which must be kept in mind if the fight against material poverty is to be effective in the long term.[13]

Democratic capitalism is certainly worthy of support when it is based predominantly on markets and incentives driven by scarcity, a democratic state, and a moral and cultural system that is diverse and open-minded. The free-market system fosters economic growth, social mobility, and self-reliance. Political liberty introduces diversity, democracy, and the idea of a constitutional government. The moral-cultural system is supported by the structures of family, Church, and other civic-minded associations. The key component of democratic capitalism is freedom.

No other system has produced an equivalent yield of benefits that have also achieved the loosening of the bonds of the feudal class culture. Yet, as Novak points out, the reality of sin must always be considered as part of the ongoing evolution of man, as we structure ourselves and measure our intentions. Let us also keep in mind that diversity is an integral element in the process of healthy capitalism. As much as we can become frustrated with the polarizing and overtly influential reporting of our free press system, it is a vital element of the democratic capitalism project. Diversity of culture, skill sets, and opinions helps fragment a society and check its power, preventing it from forming homogenous groups that may desire to overwhelm and dominate the marketplace, leaving the minority with less opportunity or worse.

An amazing by-product of democratic capitalism is that it produces not only wealth but also virtuous people whose worldly enterprises can and do complement the work of God. As history demonstrates, capitalism is able to convert an individual's talent and ambitions into the creation and distribution of wealth, and subsequent benevolence toward those less fortunate. In fact, according to the Philanthropy Roundtable, charitable giving in the United States has increased 3.5 times over the past sixty years, adjusted for inflation and population growth.[14] This is an extraordinary and grace-driven by-product of income surplus, driven by our market economy and the productivity and ingenuity it has cultivated.

From a macro perspective, the American democratic economic experiment has worked masterfully. We are an extremely wealthy nation that historically has been supported by a strong middle-class workforce. Our society was founded on the principles of religion and natural moral law. We have had all the critical elements defining capitalism for the common good (see page TK) in place to allow for large-scale success.

However, as we look into the twenty-first century, do we continue to meet the basic criteria for a successful economy that benefits the vast majority of its citizens? As society has become increasingly secular and its emphasis on civic organizations and extended family connections has diminished, can we sustain the American experience?

Our society is predisposed toward individualism and the fear of scarcity. What happens to mankind without the guiding principles of religion, natural moral law, family tradition, and civic pride? This is where you and I have both the opportunity and the obligation to introduce the transforming truths of our faith to the disordered world around us.

THREE

From "Me First" to "Daring to Be the First"

Lord, you have made us for yourself, thus our hearts
are restless until they rest in you.
—St. Augustine

For most of my life, my mantra was "Me first." It was the perfect vision for a young and aggressive kid. I have always wanted to win; I'm competitive and have been this way for as long as I can remember. In fact, I hate losing more than I like winning.

Even today, I struggle with an overly competitive nature. In full disclosure, I have been known to "toss" a club after a poor golf shot, or release a rather inappropriate comment in frustration after losing a close pickup basketball game. I have certainly improved in this area of my life, but I still have to be conscious of my temperament in the heat of battle. Much of my proclivity toward an aggressive mentality in sports also transfers to business.

In the heat of battle over an idea or direction at a business meeting, that same competitive fire can emerge. Many years ago, I became so frustrated with the position of a business colleague that I called him a "complete idiot" in front of about twenty other colleagues. It certainly was not one of my finer moments.

Money, Prestige, Power Means I Win, You Lose

I have always admired the businessmen of the world, the ones I've read about in books and magazines, watched on TV, and seen in the movies over the past twenty-five years. I was in college when the movie *Wall Street*, starring Michael Douglas, hit theaters. Though Gordon Gekko was a callous, greedy scoundrel, there was an attractive charm to his presence. His character was certainly an enigma to me.

In the movie, Gekko gives his infamous speech that sums it all up:

> *The point is, ladies and gentleman, that greed—for lack of a better word—is good.*
>
> *Greed is right.*
>
> *Greed works.*
>
> *Greed clarifies, cuts through, and captures the essence of the evolutionary spirit.*
>
> *Greed, in all of its forms—greed for life, for money, for love, knowledge—has marked the upward surge of mankind.*
>
> *And greed—you mark my words—will not only save Teldar Paper, but that other malfunctioning corporation called the USA.*[15]

I remember thinking, *But isn't the point of all the education, work experience, discipline, and grit to separate ourselves from the rest for greater success?* My definition of greater success was increasing my ability to acquire more of the earth's limited resources.

For me, it meant a large stock portfolio, a nice house, and other material comforts. At work, it meant a better bottom line, greater ROI and return on assets, and greater power and influence. Looking back, much of my motivation was not just for the money, but for the challenge, the competition, and the ego boost. It was my view of life's scorecard.

I've been reading the *Wall Street Journal* since I was fourteen years old. I was raised in the business world. After receiving my MBA, I returned to the business world to make my mark. I wanted to separate myself from the crowd and prove that I was the smartest, most hardworking, most focused person around.

But as I've mentioned, despite my competitive nature, the Catholic Church has always been an important part of my life and my identity. I have rarely missed a Sunday Mass in my entire life. I never went through a stage in life when I questioned my faith. Much of my identity has always been Catholic. It is who I am and much of what I do. In my family, we celebrate rich Catholic holiday traditions and attend Sunday Mass, even holy days. I attended Catholic grade school, college, and graduate school. I really enjoyed being part of the larger Catholic family.

However, as an adult, I could never quite come to terms with the relationship between my faith and my work. Many times, I would question some of my motives or ambitions. I had a sense that something was not quite right, but I was never able or willing to figure out the puzzle. Most often, my competitive spirit could not find a way to acquiesce to the Holy Spirit. My inner conversation went something like this: *How can I be the hard-driving business leader that I've been reading about in all the books and magazines, and yet also blend in my Catholic faith? How can I make the tough decisions if I'm burdened with God's call of benevolence, compassion, and empathy? I have to make tough decisions. I have to terminate people, demote people, and negotiate hard. I'm competitive. I want to win, and if by my winning someone else loses, that's just part of business and life. It's a zero-sum game. It's easy talk about how*

business and faith can live in harmony, but the practicality of the day-
to-day grind is a whole different story. Then again, maybe I just don't
understand the "how."

If I reflect honestly, there might have been something else at
work. There are many *-isms* in Catholicism. Minimalism is one of
them. It's that voice that asks:

- What is the least I can do and still convince myself that I'm
  being a good Catholic?
- If I'm attending Mass each Sunday, isn't that enough to
  qualify?
- Do I really need to commit my entire life to Christ? Is that
  what he is asking? Because I am certainly not interested in
  being one of "those people"—the ones who seem to have no
  life outside of church.

Catholic minimalism has reached epic proportions in the
world today. There are close to seventy million Catholics in
America today. Yet most are lapsed or at best lethargic. I was in
that lethargic category—I still attended Mass, but without any
real desire to spend time or effort in the daily implementation of
the core ideas of the Gospel message I heard there.

One day I came across these words of Jesus: "He who does not
take his cross and follow me is not worthy of me. He who finds
his life will lose it, and he who loses his life for my sake will find
it" (Matthew 10:38–39).

I've spent twenty years on this reflective treadmill. At times
I've been a little confused and troubled, but certainly not enough
to change tactics. I was compelled by my work, and I lived for the
daily challenge and personal fulfillment of doing the job well. I

was also very aware of the difficulty of making a business work in such a competitive, litigious, and cutthroat environment as exists in today's culture. Maybe I was a bit afraid to move from a "me first" position to daring to be the first to really follow Jesus. Take up my cross and lose my life for Christ's sake? Let down my guard, change direction? I just wasn't ready to go down that road. Yet there was another nagging message, from Luke 12:48, that would never quite leave my consciousness: "Everyone to whom much is given, of him will much be required; and of him to whom men commit much they will demand the more."

I knew how privileged I was, and I often felt a bit of guilt about it. I came from a strong, close-knit Catholic family. I received a solid education and great job opportunities, I married my beautiful college sweetheart, and we have three healthy kids. I have been blessed beyond what one could or should expect. "To whom much is given . . ."

By nature, I am a very introspective person. I'm constantly reading, thinking, and searching for better ideas, greater meaning, and self-improvement. Yet I began to realize that most of this energy was being focused in a linear direction. Business success is where I had the most control and certainly the greatest clarity.

My wife has been my most vocal and challenging critic. Over the years she questioned my motives, decisions, attitudes, and priorities—even accusing me of being hypocritical at times. I felt she was just naive and unaware of what it takes to prosper in business today, that she knew nothing about the reality of economics and the need to be first. I thought that maybe she wanted all the benefits without accepting the sacrifice. I would tell her, "It's easy to be a Christian when you have no skin in the game and people aren't trying to steal from or sue you every day."

The concept of Catholic social justice that I understood back then was not my vision of successful American democracy, much of which is based on self-discipline and personal responsibility.

But was that just another justification for a minimalist attitude?

I own a commercial office building that had been vacant for many months without much prospect for finding a new tenant. One day, the broker called me and said he had a tenant who wanted to lease the space. But then he added that he wasn't sure I'd be willing to accept the tenant because of my Catholicism. It turned out the prospective tenant was Planned Parenthood.

I thought for a minute and then said with clarity that I had no issue with that. After all, this was business. They had to rent space somewhere. I said to myself, "It's not as if they're going out of business if I don't rent to them."

I've always been pro-life and considered myself to be unwavering on this issue. However, I had convinced myself there must be some degree of separation between work and faith, thus allowing me to justify accepting Planned Parenthood as a tenant on our property.

Thankfully, my family talked some sense into me, and a few days later I called the broker back and declined to rent the space to those tenants. It was a poignant moment for me. It was almost as if I could hear that cock crow, that same one the apostle Peter heard after denying that he knew Jesus.

The Catholic Church has not backed down from this controversial issue. The universal call to holiness that we all share as priestly people of God holds every one of us to a higher standard of living than simply following the State's civil obligation for good conduct. Pope John Paul II was very active in voicing the position of the Church on this topic throughout his papacy:

> Christians, like all people of good will, are called upon un-
> der grave obligation of conscience not to cooperate formally
> in practices which, even if permitted by civil legislation, are
> contrary to God's law. Such cooperation occurs when an action,
> either by its very nature or by the form it takes in a concrete sit-
> uation, can be defined as a direct participation in an act against
> innocent human life or a sharing in the immortal intention of
> the person committing it.[16]

Socrates said, "An unexamined life is not worth living." As I reflected upon my actions, I was disappointed with myself and wondered how I could have considered such a decision. How had my moral compass become so skewed? Certainly there was an element of greed involved. However, there was also something more—perhaps indifference or even apathy. I had begun to numb myself to truly listening to my conscience.

It is much easier to make choices in business or life without thinking about their deeper implications. Operating this way has become a cancer within our culture.

To honestly evaluate the decisions we make, developing a deeper and more complex moral rubric takes time, deeper reflec-tion, risk, and vulnerability. Looking at the decisions of life with-in the shallow guidelines of civil obedience is a much simpler path. It is certainly the path of least resistance for many, myself included.

There were other watershed moments that began to create a crack in my work-faith foundation. Specifically, there was a distinct rift developing between my wife and me. She was finding it very difficult to live with my work attitude, focus, and priorities.

I was always attached to my BlackBerry or computer, and I continually thought about work. I said that my family was my priority, but deep down, I knew it was a lie. It just wasn't reflected in my actions. I would tell myself that if I didn't keep my focus, I would jeopardize my goals, and I would certainly not be the type of leader I wanted to be. My role models were guys who worked eighty-hour weeks and traveled twice as much as I did. I would say to myself, *If she only knew the real world.*

By the summer of 2005, my wife and I were treading on thin ice. Our one-year-old son, Andrew, was a sickly child. He constantly suffered from a multitude of allergies, and the air quality of the central San Joaquin Valley caused him severe breathing problems, which led to deep congestion and an inability to sleep. We spent many nights next to him, giving him breathing treatments every few hours or just comforting him as he struggled to breathe.

Then my wife's best friend, Andrew's godmother, was diagnosed with cancer. She spent the better part of one summer in the hospital undergoing a myriad of experimental chemo procedures that left her body and mind a wreck. When she died, her loss was devastating for us; she was just thirty-eight years old.

This was a very strange period of time for my family and me. We had just spent the past decade building our family through many tribulations resulting from infertility issues. We should have been rejoicing and basking in the gift of our three children, ages six, three, and one. Instead we were emotionally exhausted and drifting away from each other and our faith.

No Coincidences

In the fall of 2005, my wife, Kaaren, and I decided to attend a Catholic conference together. We were struggling under the weight of stress and sadness in our lives, and we needed a few days of reflection, spiritual nourishment, and renewal. At this conference there was an emissary from the little village of Medjugorje, in Bosnia and Herzegovina, where it is believed by many Catholics throughout the world that Marian apparitions have been taking place for the past thirty-five years.

As the conference continued throughout the day, a rather odd feeling came over me, a feeling as unexplainable today as it was more than a decade ago. I felt an internal tug to go on a pilgrimage to this remote village in Bosnia and Herzegovina.

Over the course of the afternoon, the feeling just kept getting stronger and more pronounced. I believed it was a ridiculous thought, and I struggled to ignore it. With my work schedule and my family obligations, I could not fathom pursuing this crazy idea. I had hardly been out of the country, and certainly was not ready to go to some obscure village in Europe for a week of prayer. After the conference, I dismissed the idea for two months, again believing it to be a sophomoric and in-the-moment thought and not worthy of further pursuit.

However, the feeling of being called persisted. In early 2006, I convinced myself to call the only company I knew that offered pilgrimages to Medjugorje. They had sponsored the Marian conference that Kaaren and I had attended. As it turned out, there was a message on the answering machine stating that they were no longer doing pilgrimages because of the retirement of the pilgrimage coordinator. In a strange way, I felt relieved. This information released me from making a decision or leaving work for some crazy pilgrimage. I had done my part and at least explored the opportunity.

Two weeks later I was still restless and unable to stop thinking about going to Medjugorje. I was sitting at my desk one afternoon and spontaneously decided to redial the pilgrimage group number. This time the pilgrimage coordinator answered the phone. I proceeded to stumble and stammer, stating that I was calling even though I knew they were no longer doing pilgrimages.

She asked me why I'd called back if I thought there weren't any more pilgrimages, and I told her I didn't know. She said that a few days ago, she was able to get someone to take over for her and that the group would offer another pilgrimage in early March, during Lent. She then said something like, "I think I know why you called." I was speechless. I replied, "I'm glad you do, but I certainly don't."

As Paulo Coelho said, "It has been said that there is no such thing as coincidence in this world."[17] Maybe I really was being called.

FOUR

Pilgrimage: Who Do You Say That I Am?

To go on pilgrimage means to step out of ourselves in
order to encounter God where he has revealed himself.
—Pope Benedict XVI

In early March 2006, I left for Bosnia and Herzegovina. I was still unsure of my intention for going on this pilgrimage. I was a bit uneasy about being completely disconnected from my work and away from my family. And the truth was, I felt very skeptical of what might await me there.

My interpretation of Catholicism has always directed me more toward the pragmatic and rational, rather than the mystical. I just wasn't sure how much of the charismatic or supernatural I could take. I did not want to be in an environment where people were frantically searching for miracles or "signs." That just isn't my style or comfort zone. And I also wondered how I could possibly handle ten days without a gym or e-mails and conference calls to keep me occupied.

From the moment we arrived in a still-war-torn Sarajevo, the trip was different from anything I had previously experienced. After twenty-eight hours of travel, we loaded onto a bus for the final two-hour ride to Medjugorje. It was late at night, and we were all exhausted. I was looking forward to sleeping on the bus. I was thinking like a tourist.

Our Croatian tour guide, Miki, had other plans for me. The first thing we did upon boarding the bus was say a prayer of gratitude for the opportunity of the experience that awaited us, followed by praying the Rosary together. It would certainly be a pilgrimage, not a vacation.

For the first time in my life, I spent several hours of my day dedicated solely to reflection and prayer. One of the extraordinary highlights of Medjugorje was the Mass itself at St. James Church. There were hundreds of priests and thousands of pilgrims in Medjugorje who all had one thing in common: a desire to experience Christ in the sacraments.

There were at least ten priests and deacons on the altar at every Mass. Throughout the week, each priest would alternate being the lead celebrant at the Mass. The homilies, liturgy, and the music were filled with an awe-inspiring energy and enthusiasm. It was unlike anything I had witnessed in my local parish Mass.

Right outside St. James Church, there were about twenty confessionals, with priests listening to confessions in a dozen languages. How amazing to see people in a rush for an open seat at the ten a.m. American Mass, or waiting in line ten deep for their first confession in twenty years.

The days were spent with Mass, walks up Cross Mountain and Apparition Hill while reciting the Stations of the Cross or the Rosary, conversing with some of the visionaries, and much fellowship with other pilgrims from all over the world. The local wine was very good too! It was an opportunity for prayer, reflection, and a humble appreciation for being a part of this unified spiritual journey we call Catholicism.

I was sincerely overwhelmed by the experience, the peace, the love, the worship, and the community of Catholics—truly one faith body. The weather that week was cold and rainy, and the little room I stayed in was cramped and chilly as well, but it made no difference. I quickly embraced the fact that I was a pilgrim, not a tourist. The minor hardships just seemed to add to the spiritual experience.

In our Catholic faith, the tradition and theology of pilgrimage has a deep and meaningful history. For thousands of years, Catholics have embarked on difficult physical journeys as a means to go deeper into the spiritual core of their lives in Christ. Going on a pilgrimage indicates a desire to journey toward some greater spiritual growth through hardship, periods of solitude, self-examination, and prayer.

In the early period of the Church, people would travel for months to make a pilgrimage to the holy sites of Jerusalem in veneration of Jesus Christ. After the conquest of the Holy Land by the Muslims in the seventh century, many people shifted their pilgrimages toward Europe's holy sites such as Santiago de Compostela in Spain, and other Marian apparition sites such as Fatima, Lourdes, Knock, and La Salette.

As part of my spiritual journey, I have come to appreciate the wisdom of our tradition with regard to this ancient practice. I too have integrated pilgrimages as part of the faith plan for my life. Since my initial trip, I have been back to Medjugorje twice, while also taking similar journeys to the Holy Land, Fatima, Assisi, Orvieto, and Rome. Each trip has provided a unique opportunity to push myself outside my spiritual and physical comfort zones, and recharge my faith. I look forward to the opportunity one day to join in the tradition of thousands before me and walk the Camino de Santiago.

My life has been forever changed by those days in that remote village in Bosnia and Herzegovina. I remember my personal theme for the week was simply "Be not afraid." Be not afraid to live your faith. Be not afraid of branching out into the unknown. Be not afraid of the world's view of failure. And be not afraid to alter your life's mission.

It was there that I finally had the courage to ask myself the most fundamental question in human history: "Who do you say that I am?"

It was the question that Jesus posed to his disciples at Caesarea Philippi. It is the same question that he asks of you and me. This question is so profoundly important to mankind that it can be found in all three synoptic Gospels (Matthew 16:13, Luke 9:20, Mark 8:29). I have realized that if we get this question wrong, it is impossible to understand our essential purpose and ever be in right relationship with our Creator. It is certainly the central question of our lives.

Reflecting back on the arbitrary events that led me to Medjugorje and beyond, I am awed by the determination of the Holy Spirit in my life. I simply can no longer believe in coincidence. There have been so many opportunities to take a different path in my life over the past decade. Yet, somehow, I am continually pulled back to the power of my experience in Medjugorje and the fundamental question of our lives: "Who do you say that I am?"

FIVE

Realizing Our Christian Identity

We can believe what we choose. We are answerable
for what we choose to believe.
—Cardinal John Henry Newman

"Who do you say that I am?"

After Jesus poses this provocative question to his disciples, St. Peter responds, "You are the Christ, Son of the living God." Peter has realized that Jesus is the anointed one, the long-awaited Messiah of Israel. Jesus responds to him, "Blessed are you, Simon Bar-Jona! For flesh and blood has not revealed this to you but my Father who is in heaven" (Matthew 16:15–17).

Jesus can never be accused of being oblique, and he does not mince words. Here he makes a definitive claim to be the Messiah, the anointed one, and by doing so he is forcing us to make a choice in how we see him: He is either who he claims to be, or he is a lunatic or a liar.

British novelist C. S. Lewis captures the radical nature of Jesus' assertion in the following excerpt from *Mere Christianity*:

> I am trying here to prevent anyone saying the really foolish thing
> that people often say about Him: I'm ready to accept Jesus as a

great moral teacher, but I don't accept his claim to be God. That is the one thing we must not say. A man who was merely a man and said the sort of things Jesus said would not be a great moral teacher. He would either be a lunatic—on the level with the man who says he is a poached egg—or else he would be the Devil of Hell. You must make your choice. Either this man was, and is, the Son of God, or else a madman or something worse. You can shut him up for a fool, you can spit at him and kill him as a demon, or you can fall at his feet and call him Lord and God, but let us not come with any patronizing nonsense about his being a great human teacher. He has not left that open to us. He did not intend to.[18]

"Who do you say that I am?" ➡ *"Who do I say that I am?"*

When you and I accept the reality of Jesus' identity as the Son of God, logic then impels us to ask the same life-altering identity question of ourselves. "Who do I say that I am?" This is the entryway and opportunity to discover our true nature, our Christian anthropology. For if we believe in the nature of Jesus Christ and God the Father, we must accept his claim upon us as well.

God created man in his own image, in the image of God he created him; male and female he created them. (Genesis 1:27)

See what love the Father has given us, that we should be called children of God; and so we are. (1 John 3:1)

For we are his workmanship, created in Christ Jesus for good works which God prepared beforehand, that we should walk in them. (Ephesians 2:10)

And if [we are] children, then heirs, heirs of God and fellow
heirs with Christ. (Romans 8:17)

But you are a chosen race, a royal priesthood, a holy nation,
God's own people, that you may declare the wonderful deeds of
him who called you out of darkness into his marvelous light.
(1 Peter 2:9)

The defining characteristic of humanity is that we are made
in the image and likeness of God. We have been created out of
his freely given love for us. God has provided us with an intellect
and a will. We are distinctly human because we possess this dual
capacity of intellect and freedom of ownership over our will.

Man is unique in his ability to harness both intellect and will,
allowing him to make rational decisions in right relationship
with his nature.

Being in the image of God the human individual possesses the
dignity of a person, who is not just something, but someone.
He is capable of self-knowledge, of self-possession and of freely
giving himself and entering into communion with other per-
sons. And he is called by grace to a covenant with his Creator,
to offer him a response of faith and love that no other creature
can give in his stead. (*CCC*, 357)

However, when we separate the intellect and the will, it leads
to a lessening of our humanity and impacts our ability to make
the decisions that place us in right relationship with God.

Currently, the most obvious example of the dichotomy between the intellect and the will is the pro-choice movement. Hu-

manity has chosen to separate the intellect from the will in order to justify the termination of an unborn human life.

The sophistication of today's science has proven repeatedly that even at conception, the zygote is a completely unique living organism. Even at this point of its evolution, the zygote is in full possession of its own set of DNA that is separate from that of its parents. Within the first trimester of pregnancy a routine ultrasound confirms visually the fact of a living and active human person. Furthermore, the developing embryo has a heartbeat and its own circulatory system just twenty-two days after conception; at twenty weeks, the baby in the womb is capable of hearing and recognizing a voice, and can respond to other external stimuli. This is all scientific fact, not opinion. It is man's use of his rational nature. As G. K. Chesterton said, "Fallacies do not cease to be fallacies because they become fashions."

Yet many will ignore the intellect in favor of the will in order justify their decision to terminate a pregnancy. Thomas Aquinas argued that the will and the intellect are partners, and freedom must be consistent with the truth. Man must utilize his rational intellect to find and understand the truth, rather than simply asserting the will in order to justify his actions.

When humanity says, "I have a right to choose," it is simply applying a philosophy of voluntarism to justify a desire to abort a living baby because of circumstance. It is the systematic favoring of the will over the intellect. In essence, if I desire it to be true, I can make it true. This is also the modern philosophy of moral relativism, which supports and promotes a society to live without any concrete universal or knowable moral truth. It is a perspective that believes the individual's version of truth that suits or justifies his or her desire is all that matters.

This is critical because man cannot possibly understand his true potential until he understands foundationally who he is as a human. Ultimately, intellect leads to knowledge, and will leads to the capacity to freely love. This combination of knowledge and love is what allows a person to be truly free.

However, our Christian reality calls us to a much deeper understanding of intellect and will than simply freedom for ourselves. The real questions are: Freedom from what? Freedom for what purpose?

The Law of the Gift

St. John Paul II said, "For we are at our best, we are most fully alive and human, when we give away freely and sacrificially our very selves in love for another." This is what it means to be a fully functioning person.

Personhood

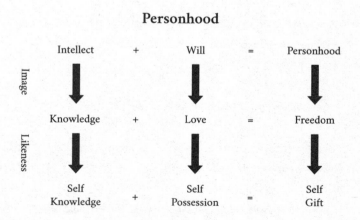

Source: The Augustine Institute, Theology 504: Moral and Spiritual Theology, Dr. Michel Therrien, PowerPoint slide.

Our intellect leads us to reason, knowledge, and ultimately self-awareness. Our will allows us the capacity for choice and enables us to love and be loved, and to choose our unique life's path toward self-possession. We possess freedom because we have the capacity to harness our intellect and free will.

Our Christian reality is about not just our personal freedom, but a freedom that dares to attain something much greater beyond ourselves. We can find many examples of our intended reality as human beings made in the image and likeness of God throughout Catholic doctrine. In *Gaudium et Spes* (*Pastoral Constitution on the Church in the Modern World*) we are told, "Man cannot fully find himself except through the gift of self."[19] There are many more instances in the Bible, such as these:

> Whoever seeks to gain his life will lose it, but whoever loses his life will preserve it. (Luke 17:33)

> A new commandment I give to you, that you love one another; even as I have loved you, that you also love one another. (John 13:34)

> You shall love your neighbor as yourself. (Matthew 22:39)

Bishop Robert Barron describes a significant issue plaguing our world today:

> One of the most fundamental problems in the spiritual order is that we sense within ourselves the hunger for God, but we attempt to satisfy it with some created good that is less than God. When we try to satisfy the hunger for God with something less than

God, we will naturally be frustrated, and then in our frustration, we will convince ourselves that we need more of that finite good, so we will struggle to achieve it, only to find ourselves again, necessarily, dissatisfied. At this point, a sort of spiritual panic sets in, and we can find ourselves turning obsessively around this creaturely good that can never in principle make us happy.[20]

Take a moment and reflect upon the reality of Bishop Barron's words. How do they relate to your understanding of Christian reality and your essential purpose? How often do you get caught up in trying to satisfy the hunger for God through worldly means?

At this stage in my life, I should know what would satisfy my desire for happiness. But I still fall into the trap of seeking substitutes for this happiness. Thomas Aquinas said that the four typical substitutes for God are wealth, pleasure, power, and honor. I am . . . guilty, guilty, guilty, and guilty!

Almost every day I have an internal battle with myself over the substitutes for God's happiness. It doesn't mean I shouldn't pursue certain goals or desires for my life. But I'm learning that I must always be vigilant about putting these pursuits in their proper context of my life's fundamental goal.

There are times when the things you enjoy pursuing (and are good at) may lead to wealth, pleasure, power, and honor. But with a deeper understanding of yourself and the ability to reflect on your actions, you can differentiate the material rewards from the reality of your essential purpose and use your gifts in a meaningful way.

The Parable of the Bags of Gold

In one of Jesus' parables, he describes what various servants do with the gifts they've been given by their master:

> For it will be as when a man going on a journey called his
> servants and entrusted to them his property; to one he gave five
> talents, to another two, to another one, to each according to his
> ability. Then he went away. He who had received the five talents
> went at once and traded with them; and he made five talents
> more. So also, he who had the two talents made two talents
> more. But he who had received the one talent went and dug in
> the ground and hid his master's money. (Matthew 25:14–18)

The parable continues with the master eventually returning home to evaluate the stewardship of his servants. When he
discovers that the servant who received one bag of gold simply
chose to bury it rather than at least attempt to invest, the master
calls him a "wicked, lazy servant!" He proceeds to command his
men to "throw that worthless servant outside, into the darkness,
where there will be weeping and gnashing of teeth."

The point of this passage is a rather stark example of what Jesus wants from us and our talents. Simply put, he wants a return
on his investment. He has given all of us unique and powerful gifts
for the benefit of ourselves and mankind. So often we choose not
to invest our time, talent, and treasure because of complacency,
greed, insecurity, or fear. This parable is a warning: God is calling
us to live our lives boldly! Dynamic Catholic's tagline is "Be Bold.
Be Catholic." It is so fitting for our faith. I know that if and when
I allow myself time for self-reflection and self-awareness, it will
lead me away from seeking the temporary happiness of a life determined by moral relativism, and instead toward boldly daring
to use my gifts for the common good of mankind.

SIX

A Novel Perspective: Work as Vocation

For whoever would save his life will lose it, and whoever
loses his life for my sake will find it.
—Matthew 16:25

Shortly after returning from my pilgrimage, I read a profile in a business magazine about the CEO of one of the largest corporations in the world. The article told of him working eighty hours a week for twenty years to reach the coveted position of chief executive officer. I remember doing the math in my head: That's 11.5 hours a day, seven days a week. In the article he also mentions taking his eighteen-year-old daughter off to college, with the irony of it all completely escaping him.

For the first time, I saw the story of a successful businessman totally dedicated and absorbed by the job in a new light. I finally had the clarity to see that this life was not for me. It all finally clicked. Saying no to this kind of life would require a deeper yes, a clearer understanding of what is truly important.

Unless you're St. Paul on the road to Damascus, life typically doesn't change radically in an instant, a week, a month, or year. My life and my attitudes weren't just magically altered either. Yet I had acquired a greater vision of what God was calling me to be. I heard a universal call to holiness designed specifically for me.

To have the courage to leap into the disruption of a life in Jesus Christ, we must truly understand our essential purpose. We must know our Christian anthropology. This anthropology is never about scarcity and fear, but always about investing ourselves in a life of spiritual abundance in partnership with a God who does not compete with humanity.

However, in order to experience our rightful abundance, we must be able to see ourselves as children of God and so choose to accept this relationship. His abundance is defined by love, not by our notions of scarcity, or whether we possess the material items that are subject to supply and demand.

The survival mechanism that sees the world through the prism of limited resources can have a profound effect on how our attitude is shaped, turning it away from the optimism and hope of happiness through God and toward pessimism and cynicism of competition for limited resources.

If we see the world through the prism of scarcity, then as soon as we feel threatened by something we perceive will limit our ability to survive, we turn away from the benevolent and optimistic nature of hope. We become burdened by the fear of potential future events that carry the possibility to alter our earthly abundance. We become obsessed with the notion of scarcity and what that might mean for our limited view of happiness.

A Shift in Perspective

You must realize now, more clearly than ever, that God is calling you to serve Him in and from the ordinary, secular and civil activities

of human life. He waits for us every day, in the laboratory, in the operating theatre, in the army barracks, in the university chair, in the factory, in the workshop, in the fields, in the home and in all the immense panorama of work.
—St. Josemaría Escrivá

In 2006, author Matthew Kelly emailed me an early draft of his new book, *The Dream Manager*. He had just spent a month in solitude walking the Camino on pilgrimage, and had been inspired to write a book about this idea of work as a deeper vocation. The book is a parable of sorts, written about a fictional company with a high percentage of unskilled or first-time employees in a very labor-intensive and service-oriented business. The company is plagued with low morale and high turnover, thus costing the company a tremendous amount of money in lost productivity, hiring costs, and training hours.

Knowing my background and experience as the owner of multiple McDonald's restaurants as a franchisee, he was looking for some feedback regarding the book's premise and ultimate conclusions.

If I had received the book five years earlier, I would have dismissed its premise as unrealistic and a bit naive. However, I had recently started to rethink my life's mission and my ultimate purpose as an employer, father, and husband.

I had just read the book *Ordinary Work, Extraordinary Grace*, by Scott Hahn. This book encouraged me to understand that my work must be integrated into my spiritual life, as one more opportunity to serve God and his kingdom. With that mind-set, I was profoundly impacted by Matthew's book. While reading it, I could feel butterflies in my stomach as the fable evolved.

Matthew's story centers upon a company dealing with serious problems of high turnover and low morale. This was certainly something I could relate to as a franchisee in the quick-service industry. The managers begin to investigate what really drives the employees' satisfaction. What they discover is that their employees' main motivation is not necessarily the promise of a bigger paycheck or title, but rather the actualization of their dreams.

More often than not, the employees have neither the vision nor the opportunity to dream. Most of them are stuck in a world focused on day-to-day subsistence. Whether it is struggling to find daycare, transportation issues, dealing with relationship strife, or simply a lack of discipline, the employers recognize that these are their employees' barriers to dreams. That is why issues with productivity or turnover can never be solved until employers can assist the employees in addressing the immediate problems of their daily lives.

Until we find the ability to overcome the hurdles of our basic needs, dreaming of a more robust life is impossible. *The Dream Manager* chronicles how the management team assembles a program using company resources to individually and collectively address the immediate needs of their employees, while also teaching them to dream.

The book's vision certainly hit home. I live in a community that faces a multitude of social and economic issues that manifest themselves in the workplace. I could fundamentally relate to the story line, people, and problems this company faces.

Instead of seeing these issues in the light of negativity and dysfunction, I began to see them as a business and personal opportunity for me. I believe we have always been a very fair employer and certainly strive to create a functional, safe, and fair work environment. It's my intent as a McDonald's franchise owner to be very mindful of our civic responsibility, and I certainly have taken on the hardships of employees.

However, this story's message goes far beyond the basic notion of "good employer." The book challenges the reader to "be not afraid" to confront the employee-employer business model relationship that permeates our economy. It is a model that simply evaluates and recognizes the employee within the context of how he or she performs in the work environment. However, the model does not pay much attention to the issues of daily life for people of a certain socioeconomic level.

Yet, if employees face issues with transportation, housing, or childcare, these problems will eventually cause problems in the work environment. Of course, the easy solution would be to terminate their employment or accept their choice to quit, and not really pay attention to the hidden cost of this turnover.

The problem is that I paid attention to these hidden costs. I knew what we were paying to maintain this model. But having the courage to change is something else. Becoming physically and emotionally involved with the daily struggles of your employees can bring on its own challenges and disappointment. Over the course of the past decade, I have certainly experienced an abundance of both. Committing time and resources does not always guarantee success or gratitude.

After I read the book, as a company we committed to supporting the Dream Manager program within our McDonald's franchisee organization. Since that time, we have consistently dared to incorporate the concepts into our daily managerial process and mission objectives.

While this hasn't always been easy, we have been a part of some incredible success stories. Getting to know our employees at a deeper level and using our resources to help their lives have been the most rewarding parts of my job over the past decade.

Today more than ever, I see McDonald's as a unique and wonderful bridge for our employees—a bridge to a long-term career with McDonald's or to college, a short-term help for family, or simply another job opportunity. When we are thinking about the needs of the employee first, we find the by-product to be greater dedication, productivity, and loyalty to the McDonald's brand and our customers.

I know much of my paradigm shift on the integration of my faith into my business would never have been possible without my initial pilgrimage experience in Medjugorje. That experience was the catalyst that allowed me to "be not afraid" and dare to truly think differently about my role and responsibility as a Catholic leader in our culture today. It is responsibility that demands magnanimity—a virtue I had not applied to my life until then.

Magnanimity is a desire to push toward greater achievement morally, spiritually, physically, and mentally. More important, it is truly desiring that same success for others as well.

The perpetual challenge for any business leader is the communication of a vision. Today, I spend a large portion of my time applying my philosophical approach to business through my actions and words. In order to be truly successful on our mission, I need all key stakeholders to buy in and help us execute the vision, every day and in each of my restaurants. We simply cannot be successful in this endeavor unless all our supervisors, general managers, and department managers buy into the philosophy of being magnanimous leaders.

The most powerful question of my life has continued to be "Who do you say that I am?" My journey to find the answer has profoundly redirected my life. Using the platform of my work as a vocational opportunity to live my faith has created a synergy to allow me to see the work-life equation through a fundamentally different lens. Now, using the insights I've gained, I believe the possibilities are endless.

Whether it is thinking differently to help our employees obtain access to college through scholarships and application assistance, providing access to computers for their children, helping them learn financial skills for their future, helping them address transportation barriers, or simply accommodating their schedule needs, it has all become part of our collective job responsibilities.

Living a Culture of Catholicism

My pilgrimage opportunities have opened my eyes to the significant loss of Catholic culture we are experiencing in the Western world. When you are enclosed within the current Catholic environment of many of our parishes or Catholic schools, it is easy to assume that this is just the way it is; it's not supposed to be inspirational, charismatic, or motivating—it's just church.

Yet, so often, what I have heard and experienced on pilgrimages and attending conferences is the exact opposite perspective. Both the priests and the laity constantly comment on the overwhelming sense of community and shared ideology that is experienced in environments such as Medjugorje, Fatima, the Holy Land, and local eucharistic or Marian conferences. It is an understanding of who we truly are as a people made in the image of God. It is a shared ideology that bonds us and unifies us toward a common vision and philosophy of life.

As the United States continues its ambivalence toward God and natural moral law, we see a society moving toward greater fragmentation, and an unraveling of the unity that once was the fabric of the American democratic success story.

As John Adams, the second president of the United States and one of the architects of the United States and its constitution, stated in 1789, "Our constitution was made only for a moral and religious people. It is wholly inadequate to the government of any other."

In the original American democratic experiment, there was a shared sense of moral values, patriotism, and work ethic. Today we cannot find a common ground that allows for collective identity, unity, and collaboration. Our inability to rally around a shared vision of America may ultimately lead us toward the historical path of the once-great Roman Empire.

The great doctor of the Church St. Augustine wrote of this in his philosophical work *City of God*, in the mid-400s. It was a challenging time for Catholics living in the Roman Empire during this period. The decay and decline of this formerly magnificent state was becoming obvious to the citizens of Rome and their enemies as well. The critical questions of the time were "What caused the decline?" and "What or who was to blame?"

Those who adhered to the pagan faith were quick to blame the Christians, claiming that the gods had abandoned Rome because of the acceptance of Christianity in the empire in AD 325. These Romans claimed that Christians were loyal not to the state, but to this "kingdom of heaven."

St. Augustine used *City of God* to refute the pagans' charges that Christians brought about the fall of Rome. He suggested instead that the Roman Empire became weak because they gave themselves up to the moral and spiritual corruption that was accepted by the pagan culture of the day. His premise was that humankind must pursue the city of heaven to maintain a proper sense of order and civility within the context of the earthly state, which in turn leads to true peace.

In effect, *City of God* is the eternal challenge to human society. To which city does your primary allegiance lead you? St. Augustine's philosophical accounting of Rome could as well have been written for us today.

Catholic philosopher Alasdair MacIntyre has written extensively on the issues surrounding the significance of shared identity and belief in a common culture to sustain a unified and flourishing society.

In his book *After Virtue*, MacIntyre concludes that individualism and its insidious by-product, moral relativism, as a guide to truth have led to an inevitable and irretrievable loss of a common culture: "Modern society is indeed often, at least in surface appearance, nothing but a collection of strangers, each pursuing his or her own interests under minimal constraints."[21] However, more damaging is the loss of a common ethical reference point to allow for productive and healthy debate.

This reality has moral, religious, social, and economic effects that are only just beginning to permeate and fracture our American culture. The most obvious examples of this lack of a common reference point from which to begin consequential debate are the pro-choice/pro-life and euthanasia issues. Without a shared reference point surrounding the intrinsic value of a human life, all debate becomes an exercise in futility.

In the midst of a secular and temporal vision of life that hardly goes beyond our generation, how can we see the vast canvas that

God has been creating for humanity? The answer lies in seeing ourselves in the proper context of who we are as members of the body of Christ. It is a citizenship that transcends today's world of pleasure and pain, in which we see ourselves in the proper context of our Christian faith.

SEVEN

Finding Our Strength in Humility

So the last will be first, and the first last.
—Matthew 20:16

One of the great challenges of my life has been embracing the concept of Christian humility. Far too often, the confidence and assertiveness that made me successful and proficient in the tasks of my daily life eventually led me down a path toward arrogance, egoism, and insensitivity toward others.

Part of this mentality is a function of my competitive spirit and desire to win. I have always addressed life's obstacles with an aggressive and assertive self-confidence in order to be successful. Yet, as many in my life can attest, I have been less than understanding when others either fail to model this same behavior or don't find value in its ideology. It's caused strife in my personal life and in my working relationships.

However, I have come to understand that our role and responsibility as Christians must always be fundamentally rooted in the humility that I realized I lacked (and far too often still do). It is not the humility that is so often perceived as weak or feeble, but a humility of strength, confidence, and fortitude. I have realized that it is only through the prism of humility that we will ultimately have the power and grace to live our lives enthroned in this principle of self-gift.

When Jesus speaks of the last to be first in Matthew 20:16, he is simply reiterating the new role of humility in the life of a true Christian. In the fifth chapter of Matthew's Gospel, Jesus speaks at length about this new and radical way of thinking about life. In fact, in this moment Jesus purposely speaks from the Mount of Beatitudes in Galilee as the "new" Moses, a bit of symbolism that was not lost on his perceptive Jewish audience. Certainly, Moses and the Decalogue was a prefiguring or typology of these eventual teachings of Jesus in the Beatitudes.

His Sermon on the Mount was a radical extension of the original Ten Commandments for the Hebrew people. In Jesus, we finally come to a moment in the economy of salvation where God has determined that man has the capacity to grasp a deeper understanding of our essential purpose. Jesus preaches that there is a new standard required of man.

The Beatitudes, found in Matthew 5:3–11, are at the heart of Jesus' preaching. They take up the promises made to the chosen people since Abraham, fulfilling those promises by ordering them no longer merely to the possession of a territory, but to the kingdom of heaven.

The Beatitudes praise and honor the meek, the humble, and the peacemakers. It is no longer good enough to live a life of an eye for an eye and a tooth for a tooth, because that is a life fundamentally rooted in the scarcity and limitations of our biological nature. We are now being called to greatness as described by Christ in the following passage delivered just after the Beatitudes:

You are the light of the world. A city set on a hill cannot be hid. Nor do men light a lamp and put it under a bushel, but on a stand, and it gives light to all in the house. Let your light shine before men, that they may see your good works and give glory to your Father who is in heaven. (Matthew 5:14–16)

This now must become our goal. This is man's mantra for choosing to "be the first" in humble servitude and obedience to one another.

However, today there seems to be an ever-increasing propensity to choose to be "less than" or some second-rate version of ourselves. Why?

We have become a society that purposely chooses to be either too wary or too self-absorbed to be the first. Perhaps we are simply not willing to muster up the courage to vigorously pursue our God-given talent—out of either fear or mere complacency.

I am as guilty of this behavior as the next person when it comes to self-absorption or lack of humility. If I'm not vigilant about my essential purpose, I will find myself drifting into a mentality that is focused on money, pettiness, or minimalism.

Sadly, some days I can go into one of my establishments knowing full well the impact my presence and personality has upon the team, yet I fail to act. I fail to come outside myself and my own personal agenda and meet the needs of the employees in their moment.

I have found that some days, all it takes is me giving a genuine smile and hello to my employees as they are working, acknowledging my gratitude for their commitment to their effort. Some days it means sitting down and listening to an issue that seems to be holding them back from becoming more successful or content in their jobs or lives. Mainly it is as simple as being present, putting the cell phone or computer away, and having the commitment to be with them in that moment. My task-driven personality can be my Achilles' heel when it comes to recognizing immense value in these moments. Today I keep a little note on my desk and computer that reminds me to check myself. The note simply states, "Be here now."

St. Francis said, "For it is in giving that we receive." It's a paradox of life that if you want to receive, you have to be willing to give. This directly contradicts the message we get from our culture, which teaches us that we are the center of everything. *Give me. Let me have it. I want to possess your life!* How many relationships are dysfunctional because of this desire to possess rather than give in selflessness?

The one thing that is impossible to do with the divine life is to possess it. Why? Because the divine life is a life of love, and true love means self-giving. Real love is about giving it away. To have the divine life is to have love in you, and to desire to give away what you have received. By giving you will have it. You will have divine life in the measure you give it away. And this will lead to the death of being "less than," of self-absorption, apathy, and pettiness. In its place, becoming a self-gift (giving yourself away) will bring the abundance and prosperity we all seek.

EIGHT

The Power of Christian Hope

Where there is hope, there is faith.
Where there is faith, miracles happen.
—Author Unknown

At Sunday Mass one weekend an obscure reading from the prophet Habakkuk affected me intensely. I listened to the reading and then read it to fully absorb its message. Take a moment and read this passage before continuing in this chapter.

How long, O LORD, must I cry for help
    and you do not listen?
Or cry out to you, "Violence!"
    and you do not intervene?
Why do you let me see iniquity?
    Why do you simply gaze at evil?
Destruction and violence are before me;
    there is strife and discord. . . .

Then the LORD answered me and said:
    Write down the vision;
Make it plain upon tablets,

so that the one who reads it may run.
For the vision is a witness for the appointed time,
    a testimony to the end; it will not disappoint.
If it delays, wait for it,
    it will surely come, it will not be late.
See, the rash have no integrity;
    but the just one who is righteous because of faith shall live.
(Habakkuk 1:2–3; 2:2–4, NAB)

In the midst of our incredibly turbulent and dark times, the distress and frustration conveyed in the words of Habakkuk seem so relevant to our twenty-first-century existence. "How long, oh LORD, must I cry for help and you do not listen?" Why is it that God doesn't seem to listen to those in Syria or Lebanon or anywhere ISIS persecutes? "Why do you let me see iniquity? Why do you simply gaze at evil?" Why must we hear and read about corrupt priests and politicians and never-ending gang violence?

How often do we fall into this way of thinking in our lives? How often do we cast away hope only to have it replaced by discouragement, apathy, and despair at the loss of our God in today's culture?

But then, God's beautiful response to Habakkuk reminds us of his grander vision and time frame. "See, the rash have no integrity; but the just one who is righteous because of faith shall live." This is God's eternal message for mankind throughout salvation history! He implores us to grasp patience and hope built on trust in him and his time.

The Book of Habakkuk was written just prior to the imminent Babylonian invasion of modern-day Israel in 605 BC. Habakkuk's prophecy was directed to a world that was again faced with looming disaster. Another powerful foreign army was invading Judah, and the people, like Habakkuk, were wondering what God was doing to protect his chosen people and the land he had rightfully given them. So much evil and death surrounded them, but it seemed God remained strangely silent. Habakkuk was asking the age-old question: Where is God? How long will he allow this pain to continue? Where is the justice?

The Book of Habakkuk reminds us that while God may seem silent and uninvolved in our world, he always has a plan to deal with evil, pain, and loss as well as goodness. Eventually, justice is always served. The example of the prophet Habakkuk encourages believers to wait for the Lord, expecting that he will indeed work out all things for our good in time. It is the everlasting message of hope.

The Book of Habakkuk teaches us that no place is too dark for God's grace to penetrate when we have faith that reaches above and beyond mere human reason. Faith must be an attitude of trust in the presence of God. Faith gives us the power that unlocks the doors to hope and optimism for an uncertain future. When we have faith and hope, we acknowledge that we are not in control, but we can still move forward in fidelity to his will. A world without God is a world without hope (see Ephesians 2:12).

Thomas Aquinas defines hope as "a future good, difficult but possible to attain . . . by means of the Divine assistance . . . on Whose help it leans."[22]

God is the source and object of our faith, hope, and love (what we call the theological virtues). The "highest" good we hope for ourselves, of course, is everlasting happiness in God's presence. We must see hope in the proper context as it relates to the kingdom of heaven. We can be hopeful even in the midst of chaos because our faith allows for us to see through the current secular battle that is raging around us to understand that the war has already been won via the promises of the paschal mystery. I'll share my own story of hope.

A Decade of Hope

My wife, Kaaren, and I were married in the summer of 1992. When we were just beginning to think about starting our family, Kaaren was diagnosed with severe endometriosis, a disorder that thrives on estrogen; the more it is exposed to the hormone, the more it grows and causes internal scarring. We learned that achieving pregnancy with endometriosis is extremely difficult.

After several appointments with doctors at UCSF Medical Center, the consensus was that Kaaren needed surgeries to help clean up the endometriosis, and then we needed to pursue pregnancy immediately. The doctors feared that if we waited, Kaaren's odds of conceiving a child would be extremely low.

Thus began a laborious journey that would be filled with many surgeries, infertility treatments, pain, and much sorrow. It turned into an odyssey that would last for the next thirteen years. From 1992 to 1997, Kaaren underwent several surgeries and a myriad of infertility procedures. We went from a young and enthusiastic married couple to a pair of harried, frantic, and bickering young adults trying to come to terms with physical and emotional pain, surgeries, and the distinct possibility of a life without the children we had envisioned having.

Unfortunately, neither of us was equipped to deal with the consequences of our situation. We were in an emotional and physical dogfight that required our full commitment and partnership. At that point, I had neither the emotional bandwidth nor the maturity to provide the support Kaaren needed. She was in a new and challenging job, living in an unfamiliar town with few friends, and with a husband who wanted to focus on his own career opportunities, learning the game of golf, and playing basketball.

By the winter of 1995, our marriage was in shambles and our lives were an emotional mess. Shortly before Valentine's Day 1995, Kaaren and I separated. We had seemed to be the idyllic young couple with the brightest future imaginable just a few short years before. It was a surreal time for both of us. Kaaren and I were separated for six long months. However, through much work, we developed a stronger commitment to each other and our marriage vows. We would certainly need that sacramental commitment in the years to come.

God Writes Straight with Crooked Lines

After repeated failed infertility treatments, Kaaren and I finally decided to pursue adoption in mid-1997. It was not what we had originally hoped for when dreaming about our future family, but over time we embraced the idea as another adventure and God's will for our lives and those of others.

As thousands of couples can attest, adoption is a very difficult process. We were involved in several domestic adoptions over the course of two years that eventually ended in frustration and disappointment. We seemed unable to make the right domestic adoption connection that would lead us to becoming parents.

During this time, we had several vigilant prayer warriors fighting on our behalf. My parents traveled to the Holy Land in 1996. While in Israel they visited the holy and ancient monastery on Mar Saba overlooking the Kidron Valley. The monastery dates back to AD 483 and has continuously had monks living there for more than fifteen hundred years. It was the home of St. John of Damascus, and it also contains the relics of St. Sabbas. In keeping with thousands of years of tradition, only men are allowed inside the monastery. Therefore, only my father and other men in their pilgrimage group were able to enter the monastery and interact with the monks.

While we were inside this ancient monastery, a monk asked my father if there was anything he would like the monks to pray for on his behalf. My father told him about Kaaren's health issues and infertility. The monk casually mentioned that when a person drinks tea made from a palm leaf at the monastery and is anointed with special chrism oil, through the intercession of St. Sabbas, a miracle is possible; many have been recorded throughout history.

My father is a very devout but practical Catholic. He has never searched for miracles. However, he was struck by the honesty and simplicity of this monk living a faithful life in a manner that has hardly changed for more than a thousand years. Before departing, my father went back and accepted this small gift of hope from the old monk. After reuniting with my mother outside the monastery, my father conveyed the story to her; she was equally moved by the event.

Back in the States, my mother kept the palm leaf and chrism oil in her purse, waiting for the right time to offer this representation of hope and faith to Kaaren and me. Both my mom and dad were a bit unsure of how we might react. It felt so meaningful and significant to them, but would we be dismissive and look upon them with a sardonic credulity? Or would we be open to the unbound mysteries of our Catholic faith?

It's that same feeling we all encounter from time to time when we have an opportunity to share our faith, isn't it? It's the hesitancy driven by a feeling of not wanting to be looked upon as a lunatic or an "over-the-top" Catholic. It reminds me of St. Paul's words to the Corinthians: "For if we are beside ourselves, it is for God; if we are in our right mind, it is for you" (2 Corinthians 5:13).

Shortly after returning home from their trip, my mother and father found the right opportunity to tell Kaaren and me about their encounter at the ancient monastery. We were moved not only by the story but also by their love and concern for us and our cross. We readily drank the palm tea and then were anointed with the oil of Mar Saba. It was a special moment for all four of us, and Kaaren and I were grateful for this small gift of faith and hope on our behalf.

One day in September 1998 I received a page from Kaaren during the middle of the morning. She was a special education teacher and rarely paged me during the day. I thought it was strange, so I called her back immediately. She asked if I would come home for lunch that day.

My initial thought was to say no. I always worked during the lunch hour and was not keen on driving twenty minutes back to the house for lunch. However, I agreed, figuring something was up. I arrived home to Kaaren, a bottle of champagne, a card, and two bows—one blue and one pink. I was immediately very concerned, thinking Kaaren was getting herself too emotionally connected to the next "perfect" adoption opportunity to come our way. I couldn't have been more wrong.

The hope and prayers of so many were finally answered. After almost seven long years of struggles, my wife had become pregnant. It was an overwhelming sensation of the utter goodness of God. Our hope and fidelity were being rewarded in greater abundance than we had ever expected. Matthew, our gift from God was born in May 1999.

Eventually Kaaren and I began to realize that if our hopes of more children were to come to fruition, once again we would have to look to adoption. It was certainly with trepidation that we reconvened the journey. The process turned out to be as difficult as our prior experiences, before the miracle of Matthew. We encountered several potential birth mothers who ended up being more interested in our money and a free trip to California, the beach, and Disneyland than finding a safe and loving home for a child.

In the spring of 2002, we were in the middle of yet another arduous adoption process. The birth mother wanted us to pay for her and her boyfriend to live by the beach in California until her due date. The boyfriend was in jail at that time, but was due out within a few weeks. The birth mother had already shown herself to be very unpredictable and was obviously looking for a way out of rural Texas. It felt like another looming adoption disaster story. However, the emotional nature of adoption grabs hold of you when you're so desperate for a child to call your own. My wife was very vulnerable and hanging on for dear life, beyond all rationality.

In the spring of 2002, we received an unexpected call from the little agency we had contacted back in 1997, inquiring about whether we were still interested in adoption. They informed us of an infant available for adoption in the Marshall Islands. We weren't even sure where the Marshall Islands were. I vaguely remembered them from reading about WWII history, but I did not know a thing about their location or people.

When we received the call, it seemed like someone was throwing us a life vest just before we were swallowed into the abyss. Our immediate response was yes! As usual with our God, little did we know what that yes was to mean for our lives.

The Marshall Islands are a group of hundreds of atolls in the western Pacific in a region of the world called Micronesia. It is classified as a part of the developing world, with very high birth rates, infant mortality, and medical standards far beneath those of North America.

We found out that we were to adopt a little boy. Within a month we received a call that a little girl was also available. The agency wanted to know if we would be interested in adopting both children. We felt such gratitude already and believed God was truly acting and leading in our lives, so we immediately agreed.

During the long waiting process, we received a picture of both but little else. It is very difficult to obtain any medical history from the Marshall Islands or anything concrete about a baby's family. This may seem like a minor detail to some, but for anxious and high-strung adoptive parents it was certainly a concern, and a major leap of faith and hope.

A few months later we received a call from our adoption facilitator with some bad news. The little boy we were to adopt had been taken by his grandparents to the out islands and was no longer available to us. We were very disappointed. It is amazing how quickly one can become attached to a picture and a dream for the future. However, we were so thankful for the opportunity to say yes to the other baby—who turned out to be our Kathryn! Yet the next few months were filled with anxiety as we prayed that our baby girl would remain available. Finally, the time had come. There was a five-hour flight twice a week from Honolulu to the Marshall Islands and then on to the Cook Islands. We flew to Hawaii and then caught the flight to Majuro, Marshall Islands. The atoll is very narrow, comprising sixty-four islets on a reef that is approximately twenty-five miles long. It is a land mass of less than four square miles and contains thirty thousand people.

We visited Kathryn for the first time on the Tuesday we arrived. She was living with fourteen people in a small one-bedroom house divided by a curtain. The was no actual door on the entrance to the house, and the floor was hard packed dirt. The water came from a large catch basin on the roof of the house. Kathryn was sitting on a dirty blanket when we arrived. There were several other little children of various ages playing and drinking coconut milk.

The night of adopting Kathryn was her first night being away from her young mother and her breast milk. Poor Kathryn was in a state of shock and anxiety. To make matters worse, she was covered with scabies, a condition caused by parasitic mites that burrow into the skin and lay eggs, causing extreme itching and rash. We had been forewarned, so we had brought topical medication to begin treatment and at least relieve some of the itching. Needless to say, it was a very long and sad night for her and painful for us as well.

After a few days on the island we were ready to take Kathryn back to California. We had our official adoption paperwork and her Marshall Islands passport. Legally, that is all we needed to return. Due to a special compact agreement between the United States and the Marshall Islands, the Marshallese passport is still one of only a few in the world that allow for free travel between the two countries.

During this period, a handful of dishonest adoption agencies were illegally taking children from the Marshall Islands into the United States without proper adoption paperwork. They were then selling the children on the black market to desperate parents. That's why the Immigration and Naturalization Service (INS) was considering putting a moratorium on allowing children into the United States without going through the US Embassy in the Philippines for visa approval. Our adoption agency had assured us that this would not be a problem for us. We would have proper adoption paperwork done through a US judge in Majuro and the INS had not officially decided on a visa solution.

When we arrived at the little airstrip on Friday to fly out of the country, we were immediately denied permission to bring Kathryn back with us. Somehow the INS had been notified, and they instructed the airport personnel not to allow Kathryn on the airplane back to Honolulu. We were notified that she was not allowed to board the plane to Hawaii.

We were faced with a major dilemma. Kathryn was now officially our child and our responsibility. We could leave her to stay in the Marshalls for the next couple of months while we ventured to the Philippines to attempt to reconcile her visa paperwork. However, due to high-level terrorist alerts after 2001, the State Department was discouraging any travel to the Philippines in general. We also had Matthew at home. He was not yet three years old and couldn't be away from his mom for the next eight weeks, but Kaaren was not willing to leave Kathryn under any circumstances.

We began pleading with the official at the airport to allow us on the plane. We showed him our official adoption paperwork. We tried to talk logically to him about our situation and the fact that we'd been assured of getting out of the country with Kathryn. He said, "My hands are tied. The INS in Hawaii told me to not let her on the plane."

By this time, Kaaren was starting to become frantic and eventually started weeping with Kathryn in her arms. I continued to plead and argue with the man, begging to be allowed on the plane. I told him that once we arrived in Hawaii I would deal with the INS. I continued to fight, but eventually realized it was not working. I was almost out of hope.

It was then, in total exasperation, that I began to pray the Rosary. I walked in a circle around the lobby area, my mind screaming for a solution. Kaaren was also praying, while holding Kathryn. As we prayed, the moment of departure was quickly arriving. I pleaded and begged again, but to no avail. We continued to pray while the plane was boarding. I could tell the airline official was stressed over the situation and had spoken a couple more times with the INS, but they reaffirmed their stance.

With minutes left before the departure, I frantically spoke to the official one last time in complete and utter despair. He looked at me and said, "Just get your family and get on the plane. You can deal with them in Hawaii. I don't want to be a part of this!" I was stunned! I thanked him profusely. We ran onto the plane right before the door was closed, while all the passengers stared at us in disbelief.

We arrived in Hawaii late Friday night and approached the customs line, expecting to wait our turn. But an angry INS agent was waiting for us, and immediately escorted us out of line and to a back room for interrogation. We spent an hour in the room being interviewed by the agent and berated for our conduct.

But we knew there was little they could do now that we were on US soil with our child, who had been officially adopted in the Marshalls and approved by a US judge. The INS knew this also, which is why they were so adamant that we not get on the plane.

After the interrogation, they informed us that we would be required to show up in immigration court in San Francisco sometime in the near future to deal with the illegal entry of Kathryn in the United States. By then, we simply didn't care. We had our daughter in the United States and knew we could handle anything else that came our way.

Several months later we had not yet heard from the INS court. I was worried that if we did not resolve the issue, Kathryn's eventual citizenship would be compromised. I called the court to inquire about the original notice to appear. The clerk searched and searched the computer for the file, but ultimately could not find anything. She told me that no file existed on this issue.

I was dumbfounded. What could possibly have happened to the file? Did it disappear or just get thrown out? Eventually, with the help of our immigration attorney, Kathryn became an official citizen of the United States and of the Marshall Islands too!

A year and a half later, Kaaren and I arrived in Honolulu for the birth of our third child, Andrew. His birth mother had come to Hawaii on her Marshallese passport to have the baby in the United States. We arrived the day after he was born. What an incredible experience to be with his birth mother and grandmother during this time. We now had legal guardianship of Andrew, and he was already a US citizen!

Over the next year we worked on the adoption process for Andrew. It was a long process because we had to attempt to contact the birth father in the Marshall Islands for his approval. After the search period and administrative work, which took a year and a half, we were finally able to adopt Andrew. In the summer of 2005, the entire family flew back to Hawaii for the official adoption.

After thirteen long years of fighting Kaaren's health issues, multiple surgeries, marital strife, infertility, adoption trouble, and the INS, our family was complete! It was all we could have ever originally hoped and prayed for in our married lives. Through all the triumph and tragedy, we remained faithful and trusted in the power of God's grace. I still marvel at his goodness and the power of hope through faith. "The LORD takes pleasure in those who fear him, in those who hope in his steadfast love" (Psalm 147:11).

Living a Life of Hope

How would your life be different if you chose to "be the first" in living a life of hopefulness rather than despair or pessimism? How would your attitude and relationships be different if you truly embraced the hope that is the foundation of our Catholic faith?

Research shows that when we adopt a positive perspective and attitude about the future, it reduces our anxiety and improves our physical and mental health as well. In turn, we are motivated to actively seek improvement in our lives and become a self-gift to others. We are innately programed to transform our thoughts into the reality of our lives. Optimistic thoughts lead to positive action and a hopeful attitude.

Catholic leadership starts with a hopeful, magnanimous spirit. I have found that when I stay positive and optimistic about the people and events that surround me, others begin to absorb this optimism and embrace this spirit.

Parallel studies show that pessimism promotes apathy and depression, which are often accompanied by a sense of helplessness that feeds the depression and hinders achievement. This has become a very serious problem.

Diagnoses of clinical depression have increased tenfold in the past fifty years. Though this is due in part to more accurate diagnoses and more open-minded attitudes concerning mental illness, it is also largely a result of environmental factors that surround our secular culture and are continually reinforced by the media.

I believe we must begin to police ourselves in terms of the negativity of our culture. If Fox News is making you pessimistic, turn it off. If MSNBC makes you feel less than hopeful, choose to fast from its content. It is important to remember that the media outlets make their living on driving viewership through content. It is rarely important what type of content they provide, as long as people are willing to tune in. If we look back on the best viewership ratings over the past thirty years, we find that it is a function of negative events that then become "news" over many days. This is the business of the media and the holy grail of their success. We can choose not to be manipulated by their business plan.

The first thing we must acknowledge, although we may not want to, is that we all face times when we are very disappointed with God. We feel no different than Habakkuk. I have felt that way many times in my life, whether it was during deep and seemingly insurmountable marital strife, the disappointment of another failed pregnancy, or a failure in a business venture.

Yet, through the sacramental nature of my faith I have eventually been given some small ray of hope. Sometimes it is just enough to sustain me for a few days. In Luke 17:6, the Lord says, "If you had faith as a grain of mustard seed, you could say to this sycamine tree, 'Be uprooted, and be planted in the sea,' and it would obey you."

Sometimes my faith is as small as that mustard seed! We see this reference to mustard-seed faith twice in the Scriptures. The mustard seed is one of the tiniest seeds found in the Middle East, but the mustard plant can spread very quickly and grow to be unusually large. The point Jesus makes is that the amount of faith needed to sustain and do great things is very small. In the midst of our struggles, even if we just keep a little faith, it will eventually lead us to hope and success we could never have imagined in the depths of our turmoil.

Conveying a Vision of Hope

So often our young people don't feel hopeful about their future opportunities in America. They see the socioeconomic environment as rigged against them. Certainly the shallow messaging from our politicians only exacerbates these feelings as they wrangle for votes. Many of my employees are of Hispanic origin and believe that our form of democratic capitalism is beneficial for everyone but them. Or worse, many never take the time to thoughtfully consider their goals and aspirations for their future. So many come from homes where English is their second language and their parents have had little opportunity to advance in a career beyond manual labor.

Today, this country has so much to offer our young people. However, without the proper guidance, messaging, and direction of a parent or mentor, many of our young Hispanic men and women become stuck in a vicious economic cycle of mere subsistence or worse.

I truly believe that service and hospitality businesses such as McDonald's can provide an incredible ray of hope for so many Americans who face these realities. Whenever I have the opportunity, I preach McDonald's as an incredible bridge of hope to the future young people envision for themselves. If continuing education is the goal, we provide scholarships, flexible scheduling, and even tutoring. If someone's dream is to learn some basic work and hospitality skills, McDonald's provides a great first step toward any future career in hospitality or people management. If a career in the restaurant or hospitality industry is the hope, McDonald's has very sophisticated training programs that allow for a high level of learning and execution at every stage of advancement and complexity of the business. The beauty of McDonald's is that a person can become a very successful general manager, supervisor, or more without a college degree.

The only requirement is a burning desire to learn, work diligently, advance, and get outside one's comfort zone. The cultural opinion of McDonald's as a dead-end job is so sadly off base. The reality is that the company is truly a channel of hope for millions of Americans who need a place to jump-start their dreams.

As a Catholic business leader, I feel it is part of my responsibility to bring the virtue of hope into my business and into the lives of my employees. I am very fortunate to have the opportunity to touch thousands of employees' lives every year. It is an awesome opportunity and a responsibility that I take very seriously.

NINE

A Journey toward Happiness

What we are looking for is happiness. Not a momentary
happiness, but one that is deep and lasting and
both human and supernatural.
—St. Josemaría Escrivá [23]

It is only appropriate to talk of happiness after exploring the concept of hope. Hope is the entryway and foundation of happiness. Once we are able to grasp Christian hope, we can begin our path toward a life of happiness.

There are so many great books that describe the foundation of living a life of happiness, and they all say fundamentally the same thing: Our happiness is simply a matter of perspective. It is a function of how we see the world and of the choices we make rather than the "stuff" we have. If we choose to see the world through the eyes of consumerism or hedonism, then our path to happiness will always be tied to feelings of pleasure and instant gratification. The problem is, there is always more stuff to buy or people to compare ourselves to who have more stuff than we do.

However, if the choices we make are based on the virtues (prudence, justice, fortitude, and temperance) and a willingness to embrace delayed gratification, then we can find lasting happiness. In Catholic theology an example of delaying gratification is engaging in the practice of fasting. By denying yourself some impulsive desire, you allow your mind to begin to control your body. That's when you allow your Christian identity to dominate your biological identity.

In the experiences of my own life and working with thousands of young people over the past twenty-five years, I believe some measure of happiness can be achieved by concentrating on a few key areas. However, a caveat must be mentioned here. The pure happiness we all innately seek but never fully achieve is actually not possible on this earth. So managing our expectations must play a part in the journey toward happiness. Ultimately we are just sojourners, knowing that the everyday ups and downs we all face are leading us to something great—and this is why we can dare to be happy even in the midst of our daily struggles.

Finding Purpose and Self-Worth

Purpose and self-worth begins with first accepting the fact that we all possess the right talents and abilities that are needed to carry out the duty God has chosen us to fulfill.

> It is Jesus who stirs in you the desire to do something great
> with your lives, the will to follow an ideal, the refusal to allow
> yourselves to be grounded down by mediocrity, the courage to
> commit yourselves humbly and patiently to improving your-
> selves and society, making the world more human and more
> fraternal. (St. John Paul II)[24]

It is difficult to make a man miserable while he feels worthy of himself and claims kindred to the great God who made him. (Abraham Lincoln)[25]

We should never waste time fretting about the talent we do not possess. Wouldn't it be ridiculous for a hall of fame wide receiver such as Jerry Rice to lament the fact that he does not have the skill set to throw a football like Tom Brady? Or a masterful computer programmer who mourns his inability to sell the software to the end user? If we don't have it, then we simply do not need it.

This goes for our loved ones as well. How often do we (not so) secretly grieve the fact that our child is not better or more interested in a certain type of sport or subject in school? How much time do we spend worrying about what our children's current skill set will mean for his or her future vocation? How many of us clandestinely try to manipulate our children's paths toward a certain type of college or career that will make them happy, but deep down it's really about our own egos? Sadly, we can spend so much time thinking about and coveting other people's talents, when in fact those talents would not lead us or our children to happiness. Why? Because that is not God's unique plan. When we pursue a path of happiness based on other people's talents or desires, we will eventually be left feeling dissatisfied and unfulfilled. So often we hear of people who are completely dissatisfied with their career choice, but they now feel trapped by the investment of education and time. Many have spent the vast majority of their lives in pursuit of what others wanted for them, only to find it was never really suited to their talents or interests.

In order to be happy, we must feel like our life means something to us and others, and we must dare to believe that we are making a difference with our time and talent. Investing ourselves in this pursuit will leave us with a feeling of self-worth.

Playing "Moneyball"

Every year in my companies we develop and implement a new business theme for the year. A few years back we branded the year "Moneyball." It was a riff on the book of the same name, written by Michael Lewis. The basic concept was to embrace the philosophy of the Oakland Athletics baseball team and its development process. The general manager of the Athletics, Billy Beane, realized that it does not take a bunch of highly paid, five-star players to make a winning team in baseball. What is needed is a bunch of two-, three-, and four-star players who work together to become a five-star team.

At my McDonald's, we don't have men and women with MBAs or degrees from top colleges. We have a bunch of hard-working and dedicated men and women from a myriad of social, cultural, economic, and academic backgrounds. In order for us to succeed at the highest level, we need to complement each other's strengths and mitigate our weaknesses.

There is great hope and happiness for all of us when we come together as a team of complementary talents. We must honor and cherish each member of the team's strengths (and understand each other's weaknesses) to combine them in a way that makes the whole so much greater than the sum of the individual parts.

I tell my employees that if they have limited English skills, we'll leverage their strength in the kitchen. If they don't like administration or accounting but are incredible hospitality ambassadors,

we'll place them up front with the customers, where they can focus on service and hospitality. If they are going to school and can
only work evenings, fantastic. Their availability in the evenings
will be a strength for our dinner and late-evening business.

The concept of Moneyball reinforces the fact that we all have
something to add to make the business succeed. It is about con-
veying a sense of purpose and self-worth to each employee that
he or she is worthwhile and possesses a skill set that is integral to
our team and our success.

Many of our employees have résumés that the normal business culture deems less than adequate. Maybe it's because of a
lack of language proficiency or certain academic shortfalls.
However, the talents so many possess are highly beneficial given
the right amount of nurturing and partnership. Maybe we are a
bunch of average players individually, but together we have the
ability to win the World Series!

Family First!

*For me, the opposite of scarcity is not abundance. It's enough. I'm
enough. My kids are enough.*
—Brené Brown

I've discovered that the reality of my long-term contentment is
not predicated on things I can afford to buy or my accolades at
work. For me a measure of joy and contentment is possible only
when I grasp the "enough" that begins with my wife, children,
friends, family, and faith. It is a contentment that is based on relationships and experiences of time spent together. Yet at times
I still struggle with the application of this reality in my life. God
has blessed me with gifts to create material abundance in my life.

There are few monetary restrictions on my ability to acquire stuff. That's why I am in a constant battle with myself to come to terms with the concept of enough. I am continually practicing restraint for no other reason than to assert control over my innate tendency toward materialism and instant gratification, rather than find the joy I seek in people and experiences.

The material goods of our world come and go, and they eventually lose their luster for all of us. But the happiness built on the love within a beautiful relationship is timeless. So often successful men and women wrap their self-esteem around the power and success they feel in their work rather than their family life. At work people have to listen to us, and we tend to feel a certain measure of control that does not always happen in the messiness of our home lives and relationships. Having an enjoyable and fulfilling career is important in our journey, but not at the expense of our relationships. The reality is that success and happiness at work is a very temporal existence. Eventually, we all become less and less relevant in our jobs and are all ultimately replaceable. If I die tomorrow, the restaurants will still open at 5:00 a.m.

As leaders and those who aspire to make a difference in the lives of others, we must dare to be first in setting the standard for what it means to put family first with our actions. We cast a long and powerful shadow over our environment. What we do and say impacts how others think and act. It is a difficult task to balance the demands of a family and being successful at work. It is so easy to talk or write about but incredibly difficult to execute. But the fact that something is difficult does not give us the excuse to not put forth the effort to accomplish this balance.

One of the ways I have found to foster a family-first mentality is to encourage flexibility in the workplace. In my experience, mature and dedicated employees value a work environment that allows flexibility and trust more than any other employment benefit, including financial compensation. When you choose family first for yourself and promote this attitude with your employees, you will find an abundance of new and creative ways to remain as productive as or more productive than before.

In my company, I give my general managers and supervisors broad flexibility with their schedules and vacation time. Over the course of my career, we have had multiple key employees take anywhere from a month to six months off for a multitude of reasons—major illnesses, weddings, the birth of a child, or just a great trip in pursuit of their dreams. Invariably other people are more than happy to step up to help cover the productivity gap associated with their absence. They all do this willingly and with a good attitude because they believe in the system and its value for all members of the team. I, as well as many in our company, love our McJob, but it is only a means to a greater end. The ends we seek are functional relationships built on a dedication to our families and the legacy we hope to leave.

Embracing Restraint

It is Jesus you seek when you dream of happiness; he is waiting for you when nothing else you find satisfies you; he is the beauty to which you are so attracted; it is he who provokes you with that thirst for fullness that will not let you settle for compromise.
—St. John Paul II

Unless we are completely clear about what constitutes true happiness, we will allow the secular world to dictate a happiness that is relative to circumstances and defined by popular culture.

This culture of instant gratification, based on *pleasure* versus long-term happiness, has been magnified by the insidious influence of moral relativism in all aspects of our society.

Although this philosophy has always been around in some form or another, today we are at a unique and dangerous crossroads. Pharmaceuticals and advancements in information technology such as the Internet allow humanity to pursue destructive pleasures without the short-term dangers that were deterrents for our forefathers. The "morning after" pill, creams for STDs, instant access to pornography, and one-click purchasing have opened up a Pandora's box of complex problems.

As we say in business, there are no barriers to entry. We have always had an inclination toward concupiscence. However, prior to the baby-boomer generation, short-term pleasure seeking associated with sexuality, drug use, and consumerism was much more difficult. There was an expectation of a standard moral code of behavior, fewer goods and services available to procure, and a painful, stigmatizing outcome associated with sexually transmitted diseases, unwed and unwanted pregnancy, and indebtedness.

In today's culture there is very little stigma attached to promiscuity, drug use, STDs, poor credit, and increasing debt. Worse, there is the issue of immediate access to extremely negative influences. For example, prior to the Internet revolution, accessing pornography was impossible without leaving the house. And today, mind-altering drugs are legal in many states and available for home delivery. Contraception is now more accessible than ever before.

The message we hear through all forms of media is: Moral relativism equals real freedom and happiness.

Still, there is a universal and inescapable objective moral truth. We innately understand that certain conduct is morally wrong. Throughout culture and history, there has always been a consistent moral norm that kept the fabric of society intact.

History has shown that society must have a standard for "right" behavior. Without some form of moral equilibrium, chaos ensues. And a culture's popular opinion at a moment in time cannot justify a moral standard. Consider the events in Germany in 1938 or the United States' immoral stance regarding slavery in the 1820s. In both examples, the majority of the citizens were overwhelmingly supportive of the policies.

Where does that moral truth come from? It starts with natural moral law. It is the light of understanding God places in us, and it results from our acceptance of his wisdom and goodness. Man has been formed in the image of the Creator and therefore instinctively knows the difference between right behavior and destructive behavior.

On a macro level, humans know that murder is unacceptable, and that lying or stealing is not constructive conduct for a healthy society. We understand this intuitively without necessarily having to be taught the concept.

Additionally, we have the revealed laws of the Old Testament, including the Ten Commandments, and the laws of the New Testament, especially the Beatitudes. Lastly, we have our cultural tradition, education within our family, and our Church's teaching to provide and form our conscience.

The Judgment of Conscience

The Catholic Church defines conscience as the application of natural moral law to a particular circumstance. The conscience allows the judgment of reason to guide our behaviors so that we may seek good and avoid evil. It must be formed by a strong moral education and aided by the gifts of the Holy Spirit.

In today's state-run educational system, the process of formation of conscience has taken a backseat to teaching a sophomoric ideology of tolerance and relativism at the expense of moral standards. Worse, our schools are primarily focused on the praxis of specific skills rather than teaching a curriculum rooted in the virtuous life.

Christianity has proven that true freedom is possible only with God and the application of the virtues—prudence, justice, fortitude, and temperance. Our understanding of freedom must be directed toward the truth of who we are as children of God. Human freedom can exist only in reasoned and ordered communion with others through the application of moral law. Thomas Merton explains it this way:

> Now at last I came around to the sane conception of virtue—without which there can be no happiness, because virtues are precisely the powers by which we can come to acquire happiness: without them, there can be no joy, because they are the habits which coordinate and canalize our natural energies and direct them to the harmony and perfection and balance, the unity of our nature with itself and with God, which must, in the end, constitute our everlasting peace.[26]

There is no denying that we live in a very confusing and dynamic world, where the lines between right and wrong can be nebulous for anyone. That is why we need the grace of the Holy

Spirit and the guidance of the Church to assist our conscience in making the right choices that will lead us to long-term happiness.

Practicing Self-Compassion

I have often wondered why so many unhappy people don't make the connection between a divine relationship with Jesus Christ and their ultimate happiness. They spend beyond their means, take pills, drink too much alcohol, work day and night, or lose themselves in a sexual relationship to overcome their feelings of unhappiness. Maybe this is because developing their faith seems too simple, too boring, or just not a quick enough solution to their immediate problems.

I have a friend who has struggled on and off with alcohol, overeating, and dejection for some thirty years. He is acutely aware of his issues and the hollow nature of his tactics to solve the dilemma that holds him back from being who God desires him to be. A few times in his life, he has even had glimpses of the beauty and peace of a spiritual life in Christ. Yet, he still struggles to see the virtues and mercy of a practiced life in Christ as part of his solution. When given the opportunity to participate in the sacramental nature of his faith, he chooses another path. Why? Maybe it's because of the shame he feels about himself, or that he has no clear understanding of how merciful our God can be. Maybe it is simply the power of inertia or an underdeveloped conscience that does not provide him the fortitude to commit to a life in Christ.

Whatever the cause, he has not been able to find the catalyst to change. However, with God there is always hope. I know that when we are ready to change, our God will be ready for us. He will always be patiently waiting, just as that loving father waited and watched for his son in the parable of the Prodigal Son. Certainly, the first step comes in finding the power of God's merciful heart that leads to self-compassion.

Over the centuries the apparitions of the Blessed Mother continue to challenge us to partake in the sacrament of reconciliation. God wants us to be cleansed and begin anew. It is through this process that we can let go of all our previous transgressions and leave the yoke of our past sins behind. In places such as Fatima, Lourdes, and Medjugorje, it is not unusual to see hundreds of people waiting in line at any one time to partake in the sacrament of reconciliation for the first time in five, ten, twenty, or even thirty years. The courage it takes to overcome the fear and shame of years of sin is a special part of the resulting joy that so many millions have experienced through these special places. However, we don't need to travel to an apparition site in Europe to experience this extraordinary gift. This opportunity is available in every Catholic church across the United States and the world. What is holding us back from partaking in this sacramental experience? Maybe it's time you mustered up the courage to choose to be first and lead your family to a deeper sense of peace and liberation via the sacrament of reconciliation.

Harnessing the Power of Reciprocity

Reciprocity is our inherent willingness and desire to exchange our unique gifts with each other for mutual benefit. As human beings, we all feel a natural pull toward reciprocation. We are programmed to give and share; it is an innate human trait that is common throughout all cultures.

According to Pope Benedict XVI, "By considering reciprocity as the heart of what it is to be a human being, subsidiarity is the most effective antidote against any form of all-encompassing welfare state."[27] Our sense of empathy and compassion for others flourishes when we rely on each other through the exchange of talents and resources. It is part of our nature, and why humanity thrives in community versus isolation.

This is a gift of our Christian inheritance; we want to share happiness. Reciprocity is truly the foundation of the Church's teaching on subsidiarity. It is a theology that highly encourages the rights and responsibilities of the individual, but it also acknowledges and supports the symbiotic benefit of community. It is the community's responsibility to provide care and assistance to each other in sustenance of the common good and the dignity of the human person. However, this must not be done at the expense of the individual's right and responsibility to do her part to take care of herself. Unfortunately, too often either our collective misplaced generosity or our ambivalence clouds the importance of a capable individual's responsibility to himself in engaging in reciprocity. When this is not permitted or encouraged to transpire, it gives subsidiarity and social justice a black eye.

When the power of reciprocity is working in conjunction with our Christian nature as self-gift, we labor together as human beings for the greater good of society or business, along with the moral, spiritual, and physical growth of each of its members.

Early in my business career, when I was overly focused on daily productivity and immediate results on the job, I was never truly happy in my work. I was always dissatisfied with either the sales growth, profit margin, or operational execution in the

restaurants. This was certainly at the expense of people and relationships.

The problem was that I just didn't understand the difference
between never being happy and never being satisfied. I was never
satisfied with the results, and that mind-set made me chronical-
ly unhappy in my work. Maybe it was because of my somewhat
introverted nature, but it took some time and coaching for me
to grasp the subtle but important difference between these two
ideas.

It's certainly all right to strive for more in business or life.
Magnanimous leadership is perpetually seeking incremental improvement not only personally, but for others as well. I believe in
pushing myself and others to stretch outside our comfort zones
to reach new heights in professional development and execution.
However, that is much different from projecting a perpetually
dissatisfied attitude.

Whether you are the CEO of a company, a parent raising children, or a leader in your parish, I have come to realize that a great
leader must be a happy leader. People do not respond well to
someone who is negative, unhappy, or unpredictable in his or her
disposition. I am embarrassed to admit it, but there were years
when my employees cringed when I came through the door.

Whether it is in marital or work relationships, dysfunction
ensues when people feel like they are walking on eggshells in your
presence. It is a horrible and stressful way to live and be productive. Over the long term it leads employees or family members to
indifference, disloyalty, and deception.

I have overcome my emotional immaturity in this area by valu-
ing people first and results second. By first focusing on people instead of my own feelings of dissatisfaction with work or with my

employees, I have been able to understand how important, reward-ing, and critical good relationships are to a successful enterprise.

I have spent the better part of the past fifteen years investing in reciprocity as a business strategy. I have found that a higher level of loyalty and execution is the result, and my happiness has been its by-product.

Small Gift, Big Reward

I believe the greatest gift you can give your family and the world is a healthy you.
—Joyce Meyer

I have always believed that when you feel good about your phy-sique and implement an exercise routine in your life, you tend to be a happier and more energetic person. That's why I have always incorporated a consistent fitness routine in my life. I enjoy noth-ing more than going on a beautiful hike, riding my bike through the countryside, or jogging on a beach. No matter what state of mind I am in before I begin the activity, I am always more con-tent and happier during or after. Furthermore, many of my best ideas have come during a long run, when I am lost in the almost transcendental experience. There are very few activities in my life that have that same effect on me.

With this philosophy in mind, a few years ago I gave out about sixty Fitbit step-tracking devices to my senior management team. I thought it would be a fun way to start the year and help theme it around the importance of activity, consistency in daily routines, and the power of camaraderie for success. We began to wear the devices, and in friendly competition, we tracked each other's progress through a social media phone app.

Part of the beauty of working at McDonald's is that we are always on our feet and moving. So the more you hustle and provide quick service, the more steps you rack up. It started as a fun way to get everyone a little more focused on moving those customers and tracking our daily exercise. But more broadly and longer term, it was about getting people to see how important a healthy lifestyle and a sense of shared identity can be to our happiness.

After several years, I am proud to say that many of my employees have taken the idea far beyond anything I had originally imagined. Many of the original participants have now brought in others, including their spouses and friends. On any given weekend you can find several of our employees running a half marathon or 5K together, sharing in the power of their reciprocity.

A Final Point: Happiness Is a Choice!

Action may not always bring happiness; but there is no happiness without action.
—*Benjamin Disraeli*

The very best marriage advice I ever received was that love is a choice, not a feeling, and it's a choice that proves itself with action.

I believe the same thing can be said of happiness. We must actively seek happiness through a life dedicated to self-discipline, virtue, and the grace and wisdom of the Church. Starting today, choose happiness. Here are some of the tactics that have worked well for me as I've continued on my journey.

Be the first to radiate optimism at work and home.

Be the first to share your unique gifts with others.

Be the first to smile and say hello to a colleague or stranger.

We must have the courage to choose happiness. We must have the courage to make choices that delay instant gratification, utilize a well-formed conscience, and share our gifts. This is the hallmark of our Christian inheritance.

TEN

Discovering Joy in Sacrifice

We are never so defenseless against suffering
as when we love.
—Sigmund Freud

The path of love and self-gift leads man toward a life of joy and happiness. However, the happiness that I am referring to is a much deeper, supernatural happiness, something far beyond simply having fun. It is certainly not the modern notion of happiness, which centers on fleeting feelings predicated upon all things external—a cycle of continuous pleasure and the utter avoidance of pain and suffering. As Matthew Archbold says in his book, *Faith under Fire*:

> The simple truth is that every act of self-giving love turns the world upside down. It seems like that's the one thing the world is never prepared for. Anytime we choose to love, we invite heartbreak. Some refuse to love wholeheartedly because of this; they shy away and shun love, unwilling to risk getting hurt.[28]

Make no mistake: Happiness and lasting joy derived from self-gift does not imply a life without sorrow. At some level, the path of love and self-gift will always include suffering. The honesty of Jesus in the Gospels is a refreshing antidote to modernity's false promises that happiness is possible through an avoidance of pain and suffering.

Jesus makes his point clear in all the Gospels:

> If any man would come after me, let him deny himself and take up his cross daily and follow me. (Luke 9:23)

> He who does not take his cross and follow me is not worthy of me. (Matthew 10:38)

> If any man would come after me, let him deny himself and take up his cross and follow me. (Mark 8:34)

> I have said this to you, that in me you may have peace. In the world you have tribulation; but be of good cheer, I have overcome the world. (John 16:33)

As St. John Paul II makes clear, the path of humanity in Christ is in accepting sorrow even though we are not always capable of understanding its meaning.

> To suffer means to become particularly susceptible, particularly open to the working of the salvific powers of God, offered to humanity in Christ. In him God has confirmed his desire to act especially through suffering, which is man's weakness and emptying of self, and he wishes to make his power known precisely in this weakness and emptying of self.[29]

It is essential to understand that a single justification of the suffering we endure is not always possible, but man must be willing to look at his hardship through the eyes of Christ the Redeemer. Seeing the difficulties in our lives or those of our loved ones through the diverse lenses of charity, humility, transformation, discipline, and redemption frees us to see beyond a specific event itself. It then becomes possible to see events through Christ's example of sacrifice and redemption.

It is only through the path of love by way of self-gift that we can find the joy that leads to sustainable happiness.

A few years back, I had a young female employee, Erica. She had started at McDonald's at the age of fifteen and had worked there for the next nine years. During this time, she proved herself to be an incredible asset to the restaurant. She was an amazingly efficient and friendly employee and was well liked by customers and her fellow crew members.

Along the way, Erica used McDonald's as her bridge through high school and college. She enjoyed the job, working as she pursued her dream of being a bilingual schoolteacher. After many years, she finally achieved her goal and was hired to teach in the local school district. She had also married a wonderful young man and was pregnant with their first child. The day she put in her two-week notice, she called me to thank me for the opportunity to work at McDonald's. I remember thanking her for all the time and dedication she had put in on behalf of McDonald's, the employees, and the customers. The last thing I said to her was simply, "If you ever need anything at all, please call me. You are a special person and I know that life has great things in store for you."

It wasn't more than a couple of weeks later that I received a call from her in a state of panic and shock. The night before, her husband, Ernie, had been in a terrible accident. He had been working with a friend, helping him build his house. After a hard day's labor, they'd had a few beers to relax. That night was extremely stormy, and on the way home he lost control of his vehicle and hit another car. Ernie ended up without a scratch, but the gentleman in the other car, who was well-respected in the community and the chaplain at a local federal prison, lost his life.

The news was completely devastating. There was such tragedy and loss on both sides. Erica had a wonderful new job, she was carrying their first baby, and she had big dreams for her family's future. Ernie was a faithful and affable young man who was devoted to his wife, his faith, and his job. Yet, he had acted irresponsibly and cost his family their future and a man his life.

Erica reached out to me for support and direction. Over the next four years, my wife and I supported them as best as we could during Ernie's incarceration in San Quentin State Prison. We had the opportunity to visit him on many occasions and experience his sorrow, anguish, and shame. Ultimately, Ernie served two years in prison and several more years on probation. After his release, I had the good fortune of having him work for me for a couple of years until he was in a position to resume his prior career.

It was a harrowing few years for him, his family, and the victim's family. The victim's wife was incredibly angry and bitter, as would be expected. All this weighed very heavily on Ernie, and I'm sure he carries that burden still. Yet this kindhearted man has never lost his faith in God's love for him.

Kaaren and I were honored to be chosen to walk with them on their via dolorosa, and to offer what little we could to support them and their family. I know that the experience has added long-term value to our lives and those of our children. We felt the impact that the poor choices of others had on society, we felt empathy for Ernie and Erica, we came face-to-face with the fear and financial burden of incarceration, and we felt the power of God supporting the families. The experience of their pain, anguish, and despair was of monumental benefit to many others in their life.

I know that Ernie and Erica have struggled mightily with their cross, but today they continue to persevere together and have another beautiful child to love and care for. Though we no longer keep as connected with them as we did during their time of suffering, their story and influence continues to resonate with us in myriad ways. We still marvel at their courage and commitment to one another and their utter faith in Jesus as their Savior and Redeemer.

The mystery of all our unique suffering certainly can never be fully understood by any of us. The questions that loom on this subject are much too complex for mere humans to comprehend. However, choosing a life of faith and hope has allowed humanity the ability to overcome the sorrow, anger, and despair that only leads to greater misery. How can we seek redemption and understanding in the suffering? Again we look to the wisdom of St. John Paul II:

> Christ does not answer directly and he does not answer in the abstract this human questioning about the meaning of suffering. Man hears Christ's saving answer as he himself gradually

becomes a sharer in the sufferings of Christ. For it is above all a call. It is a vocation.[30]

In many ways my father epitomizes the American dream. He was born and raised according to the poor Italian immigrant experience of the 1930s. My grandfather was an unskilled laborer from Sicily, struggling to provide for his growing family in rural Ohio in the heart of the depression. Whether it was my grandfather waiting in cheese and bread lines for a little extra food or my father and his siblings going door-to-door selling vegetables from the garden, they unified around faith, family, and survival. The family lived in a two-bedroom farmhouse with no indoor plumbing until my father was sixteen years old. He was one of the very few from his socioeconomic circle to attend college and go on to achieve a measure of wealth. He has been married to my mother for more than fifty-four years. From a macro perspective—what a life! In fact, he and my mother would be the first to acknowledge, with an almost uncomfortable sentiment, the richness and abundant blessings God has provided their life together.

However, my father and mother have both endured much pain and suffering in their lives, and in that of their extended family as well. I write of this only to make an important point: My parents have never viewed their lives through the prism of their difficult times. They would never consider defining their lives by their suffering, but there is no doubt this suffering has helped define their lives in some way. I believe this to be the profound wisdom and meaning that St. John Paul II's words reveal to us: "Man hears Christ's saving answer as he himself gradually becomes a sharer in the sufferings of Christ." We must confront and embrace his cross as a part of living an authentic Christian life. It is only through the cross that we can ever hope to fully encounter him and the true happiness and abundance we seek.

I have read St. John Paul II's theology of suffering many times, but I am still a little perplexed and uncomfortable with wholeheartedly embracing the redemptive nature of suffering. This is based partly on my own fear of what that suffering might actually mean in my life. However, in reading his words in relationship to my mother's and father's lives, I have arrived at a greater sense of clarity in his meaning that, for me, comes in seeing one's life through a wide-angle lens that captures the entire journey of a life lived in Christ.

I do know that success and victory are always much sweeter when they have come after failure or defeat. It is the benefit of perspective and life's contrast that defines our ability to discern our happiness from and in the midst of our suffering.

ELEVEN

Living a Legacy Today

As each has received a gift, employ it for one another,
as good stewards of God's varied grace.
—1 Peter 4:10

For we are [God's] workmanship, created in Christ Jesus
for good works, which God prepared beforehand, that we
should walk in them.
—Ephesians 2:10

The reality is, we all want to feel that our lives matter to someone in this world. Deep down, we want to feel that we have accomplished something beyond self-gratification. The desire to leave a legacy is in everyone's DNA. It is part of the innate longing we have to reach the fullness of our Christian nature we call self-gift. It is the epitome of true prosperity and true abundance.

St. Thomas Aquinas noted almost nine hundred years ago that God provides us with the gift of intellect and will, as well as the efficacy of prayer. With these unique gifts, given only to mankind, you and I can make a difference! We have the power to change the world.

Ultimately, to create the legacy that we all desire for our lives, we must see our time on earth through the prism of *contribution*. This means our lives must be used as a vessel to provide our unique gifts to others. Our Christian faith teaches us that the act of self-giving will lead us on our path to joy and happiness. The use of our intellect and will to contribute our best gifts to others is the true and holy evolution of what makes us human beings. As Bishop Robert Barron says, "Your being increases in the measure you give it away."[31]

Unlike the model of success or failure based on an economy of scarcity and competition, a life of simple contribution does not need to be scored or measured. Contribution as self-gift can be truly measured only in the transcendent world of God. It is he, not the institutions or social norms of the world, who ultimately determines the gauge of our impact.

Thus, we are no longer burdened with some cultural litmus test imposed on us by modernity. We are defined no longer by wins or losses, but by simple contribution to others. This was Christ's message two thousand years ago in Galilee, and this is his message today. When we embrace humility and contribution, we can free ourselves to act proactively toward others in a "be the first" mentality.

Jesus told a story that illustrates this principle of contribution and true abundance:

> And Jesus sat down opposite the treasury, and watched the
> multitude putting money into the treasury. Many rich people put
> in large sums. And a poor widow came, and put in two copper
> coins, which make a penny. And he called his disciples to him,

and said to them, "Truly, I say to you, this poor widow has put in more than all those who are contributing to the treasury. For they all contributed out of their abundance; but she out of her poverty has put in everything she had, her whole living." (Mark 12:41–44)

This little story from the Gospel of Mark reiterates that the measure of our contributions will not be determined by the standards of our culture, but only by our heart.

Living Contribution in Business: Ronald McDonald House Charities

Ray Kroc, founder of McDonald's, famously said, "None of us are as good as all of us." That philosophy has been carried through his legacy, Ronald McDonald House Charities. The following is a great illustration of how the business world can tap into the power of contribution.

In 1972, the Philadelphia Eagles were fund-raising in support of team member Fred and his wife Fran Hill's daughter, Kim, who was battling childhood leukemia. After raising enough funds for Kim's hospital bills, the Eagles' ownership decided to continue to raise funds to benefit local area hospitals.

Dr. Audrey Evans, a pediatric oncologist at the Children's Hospital of Philadelphia, saw a need for families to stay in a supportive place while their children were in treatment for extended periods of time, essentially a home away from home, rather than stay at a random motel or commute each day. The general manager of the Eagles, Jimmy Murray, contacted a local advertising agency to explore how best to support this idea and to promote a way to raise enough money to make the idea a reality.

The agency came up with a simple but profoundly impactful idea that continues to this day: What if McDonald's would donate twenty-five cents from every Shamrock Shake sold in the region toward the purchase of a house?

Ed Rensi, the McDonald's regional president, agreed as long as McDonald's could take the name of the house. On October 15, 1974, the world's first Ronald McDonald House was born.

Today, Ronald McDonald House is supported by millions of people giving a few cents to support sick children and their families, and now there are 356 houses all over the world. Most of the support for the millions of people served each year comes from the smallest of donations from our customers, local communities, and the McDonald's owner-operators in the area of each house. Just one example of the many programs McDonald's and its independent owner-operators are involved in is this program; since 2010 McDonald's owner-operators have been donating one penny from every Happy Meal sold to Ronald McDonald House Charities. The total giving through 2016, for just this one of several initiatives, is more than $35 million.

This is a wonderful example of capitalism for the common good. In today's economy, there are many examples of great companies who have figured out how to leverage their employees' and customers' desire to be a part of the contribution game to help change lives.

Many companies today have realized that this dual mission of capitalism as a force for good resonates very favorably with consumers and impacts their purchasing habits. Another perfect example of this philosophy in action is Toms shoes. For every pair of shoes that is purchased, Toms will donate a pair to a needy individual somewhere in the world.

The Papacy and Legacy of Francis

Let us all remember this: One cannot proclaim the Gospel of Jesus without the tangible witness of one's life.
—Pope Francis

There is no denying that the early stages of Pope Francis' papacy have made many people uncomfortable. He is a Jesuit priest, but has taken the name and philosophy of an iconic monk: St. Francis of Assisi.

I believe he was chosen by the movement of the Holy Spirit in this moment in history for a unique purpose. His choice of the name Francis is significant and revealing. It demonstrates that he has come not to be a brilliant theologian the likes of Pope Benedict XVI or Pope John Paul II, but to be a uniquely pastoral leader. He desires to show the world love in action and what it means to live as a humble member of the Catholic Church. He is perpetually challenging us to live a legacy through our daily actions and our merciful hearts.

Francis is our first pope from South America, and he sees the world through the eyes of a people who have faced social and economic injustice since colonial times. He has seen the effects of unregulated capitalism and totalitarianism on his country and his people. Francis has witnessed the ravages of abject poverty and the indifference of many to the plight of those who live in it. He has become God's messenger to remind us of our obligation to each other and to systems of governance that provide opportunity for all people: "To all of you, especially those who can do more and give more, I ask: Please, do more! Please, give more! When you give of your time, your talents and your resources to the many people who struggle and who live on the margins, you make a difference."[32]

When we are bound by the fear of scarcity, we don't have the capacity to live outside a comfort zone that protects our wealth and social status. At best, living this way allows us to consider leaving a legacy with our material goods after we no longer need them. There is nothing wrong with the idea of leaving some of our wealth for others when we pass, but there is no risk whatsoever in this philosophy. It is a mentality that says, "I am going to live my life as I wish, providing for all my material desires, but if there is anything left after my passing, I would be willing to give a bit of it away to those in need." That is acting in the comfort zone of contribution.

Our ability to live a legacy is always contingent on our ability to embrace mercy and reject fear. When we dare to invest ourselves and embrace the philosophy of self-gift, we have the freedom to live a legacy today.

Providence and Dominion

A significant point about leadership in the twenty-first century is a commitment to the resources of the earth. Through the mighty works of God, we have been given providence with the earth's bounty. The provisions of the earth are a divine gift from our Creator, and they need to be harnessed and cherished through our prudent toil and stewardship. "Yet he did not leave himself without witness, for he did good and gave you from heaven rains and fruitful seasons, satisfying your hearts with food and gladness." (Acts 14:17).

Through our intellect and will, God has given man dominion over his creation, as well. "Then God said, 'Let us make man in our image, after our likeness; and let them have dominion over the fish of the sea, and over the birds of the air, and over the cattle, and over all the earth, and over every creeping thing that creeps upon the earth" (Genesis 1:26).

This providence and dominion requires stewardship on behalf of the less fortunate and our future generations.

Pope Francis' encyclical *On Care for Our Common Home*, *Laudato Si*, is directed toward business and political leaders of the world. He states:

> The ecological crisis is also a summons to profound interior conversion. It must be said that some committed and prayerful Christians, with the excuse of realism and pragmatism, tend to ridicule expressions of concern for the environment. Others are passive; they choose not to change their habits and thus become inconsistent. So what they all need is an "ecological conversion," whereby the effects of their encounter with Jesus Christ become evident in their relationship with the world around them. Living our vocation to be protectors of God's handiwork is essential to a life of virtue; it is not an optional or a secondary aspect of our Christian experience.[33]

When we are determined to find God in our chosen vocations, I believe it is possible to see everything in a new light—the light of Christ. Whether it is people or resources, the same principles of ethical behavior and virtue apply. As powerful a tool as democratic capitalism can be in wealth creation, productivity and technology advancements, and wealth redistribution, it still has its shortcomings in relation to the reality of man's fallen nature and the power of greed, gluttony, and materialism.

Once more, we need to reject a magical conception of the market, which would suggest that problems can be solved simply by an increase in the profits of companies or individuals. Is it realistic to hope that those who are obsessed with maximizing profits will stop to reflect on the environmental damage, which they will leave behind for future generations? Where profits alone count, there can be no thinking about the rhythms of nature, its phases of decay and regeneration, or the complexity of ecosystems which may be gravely upset by human intervention.[34]

I was recently in the Marshall Islands for the first time in many years. Modern amenities such as the internet, cell phones, prepackaged goods, and processed foods have reached the Marshallese people and their culture.

Today this remote island community is partaking in the technological advancements of modernity, but without the social and educational understanding to deal with its by-products. It is a society with one foot in today's world and the other planted in the mentality of an ancient island culture that does not know how to effectively deal with the advancement and aid it receives.

The teen pregnancy rate in the Marshalls is one of the highest in the world, with almost 40 percent of the population under fifteen years old.[35] Most are living without proper plumbing, sanitation, or nutrition. Furthermore, you see street after street and beach after beach filled with overwhelming amounts of garbage—plastic bottles, aluminum soda cans, and polyethylene bags seemingly everywhere. The atoll is plagued with the by-products of imported modern conveniences such as packaged goods, processed foods, taxis, and monetary aid. These by-products include diabetes diagnoses and obesity rates that are among the world's highest.

From the magical aqua lagoon to the dilapidated concrete buildings and garbage, I am reminded of the work of the great theologian Romano Guardini and his book *Letters from Lake Como*: "Technology has created an alternative universe, self-sufficient and almost independent of given nature. Technology has become our destiny that subjugates its human creators as much as their creation. Man withering behind the destructive hands of modernity."

What happens to a culture and its people when technology permeates at a faster rate than the people's ability to acclimate to its effects on society? What is the carnage of this imbalance? Today we see it not only in the Marshalls, but all throughout the developing world. Our history teaches us that progress cannot be stopped. Thus, as Guardini states, "First we must say yes to our age. We cannot solve the problem by retreating."[36]

Therefore, humanity must adjust and assimilate without losing dignity, our ultimate purpose, and responsibility to each other and our earth. Guardini also says:

> Further, it must be possible to tackle the task of mastering nature in a way that is appropriate . . . a new order of living, standards of what is excellent and what is despicable, of what is permissible and what is impermissible, of responsibility, of limits, etc., by which we can hold in check the danger of destruction presented by arbitrary natural forces.[37]

This perspective is true not only in the Marshall Islands, but in our families and work as well. Whether it is Snapchat, Facebook, e-mail, or processed foods, we must find a way to allow our ever-advancing technology to be integrated into our life in such a way that it is controlled and harnessed for the betterment of our essential purpose, rather than transforming us into something short of God's vision for us. Something as basic as fasting from technology for a period of time, finding time to exercise, and having healthy family dinners together at home can be a first step in harnessing the power of modern technology toward the common good and our essential purpose.

I know there is much controversy surrounding the positions of the United States Conference of Catholic Bishops and the Vatican on climate change and other environmental issues. We are free to disagree with specific opinion regarding the science behind global warming or some other major global issue, but we cannot deny the awesome responsibility of our obligation to our world and its future inhabitants. We do not own this land, but are only its current tenants. No sane person can deny the destructive reality of unabated technological advancement on our culture and its people. Therefore, we cannot allow one issue to be used as a scapegoat for shunning our moral obligation to harness technology in a way that honors and advances the dignity of the human spirit. This is our legacy. What are you doing within your family or community to fulfill this duty?

Living a Legacy

Legacies that matter are connected with people. A hundred years from now all that will matter is the people that you connected with in such a way that you added value and meaning to their lives.
—*John Maxwell*

Recently I gave a talk to a group of business owners about our roles and responsibilities as Christian leaders for our culture. I was asked about my desire for my own legacy. I appreciated the question because it is one that we must be continually asking ourselves throughout our entire careers. As our lives evolve and our roles and responsibilities change, so must our expectations of living and leaving a legacy. I believe one's outlook on legacy must be viewed in proportion to his or her unique and ever-changing talents and resources.

Those of us who have been given so much are morally obligated to reciprocate, as Jesus tells us when he says that much will be asked of those who have been entrusted with much (see Luke 12:48). We have all been entrusted with so much—are we going to bury it in a hole or accept with courage the responsibility of these gifts?

Ultimately I place my role as husband and father at the top of my list of responsibilities. Thus, my legacy will first be contemplated and measured based on my relationship with my wife and children. I want to live a legacy of love, respect, and accountability toward my family. If I can get this right, I will have been successful in leaving my legacy.

In the business world, if you want to live and leave a legacy, you must invest your time, talent, and treasure in people. The legacy we live in business is always about developing magnanimous leaders in our organizations who are capable of imparting our mission to others.

This doesn't mean that everyone has the potential to be the next Jack Welch or Jeff Bezos. But we want to develop people who project and provide a generous spirit, inspire others to be a little better every day, are altruistic, and are forgiving. It is only through people that we have the power to change the world, and it most often happens shoulder-to-shoulder and one life at a time.

If I am vigilant about modeling this behavior while taking every opportunity to communicate in word and deed, I am confident that my legacy will impose a culture infused with magnanimous leadership.

This same understanding of success through people must also be embraced within our community activities and parishes. People are inspired by people! We must spend energy developing partnerships with others who desire a greater sense of purpose and are willing to share in our passion and commitment. This is the only way to create a sustainable and lasting legacy.

Here are four steps you can take today:

1. Declare and *believe in yourself* as a gift and worthy of contribution.
2. Dare to make a difference by investing your time, talent, and treasure.
3. Get out of the scarcity mode of success or failure and into the mentality of simple contribution.
4. Accept that we are meant not for comfort but for greatness. Has there ever been a saint who did not accept discomfort and persecution?

From the very beginning, the Church's central message has been about legacy. It is why we are always a missionary Church. The whole point of the New Evangelization is to reassert the original mission given to St. Peter and the rest of the apostles: "Go, therefore, and make disciples of all nations, baptizing them in the name of the Father, and of the Son, and of the Holy Spirit" (Matthew 28:19).

The pivotal question we all must consider: What will our legacy be? Are we willing to step out and begin to define it today?

Let's choose to be the first to offer our time, talents, and treasure for our children and our Church.

TWELVE

Leadership at the Service of Life

Place your talents, enthusiasm, and fortitude
at the service of life.
—St. John Paul II

It has been more than a decade now since I began my journey to discover the deeper responsibilities of what God is asking of me in my vocation as a Catholic business leader. This journey has led me on a meandering path toward much greater reflection on my actions and a deeper sense of accountability for my life during my short time on this earth.

Many of the modifications I have made in my life commenced with my initial pilgrimage in early 2006. One of the crucial lessons from that experience was the importance of surrendering to a greater purpose.

"Only with total interior renunciation will you recognize God's love and the signs of the time in which you live."[38] Our Blessed Mother has been proselytizing with this message across the world through her apparitions for hundreds of years. Why does she repeat the same ideas again and again? Because she knows we need to be reminded of these messages, much like we remind our children of the same messages over and over. We need renunciation—fasting, prayer, sacrifice, denial, and obedience. When we deny ourselves, we can finally begin to gain control over the body and allow our lives to be dictated by our minds and our souls.

With each opportunity that we take to engage in interior renunciation, we gain a measure of freedom that is possible only through denial and prayer. When we are so focused on our own needs, wants, and temporal desires, we simply do not have the capacity to be the self-gift that is our essential purpose.

There is no easy way to accomplish many of the ideas that have been discussed in this book. The reality is that failure is inevitable and it's something we must all face. Continuing to move in a positive direction does not mean we will not face significant setbacks along the way. To overcome these setbacks and continue to move forward along our path toward holiness, we must be willing to embrace self-compassion as well. We are our own worst critics and worst enemies. We are all far too hard on ourselves. The self-loathing that follows our mistakes is extremely detrimental to our self-confidence, hope, and ultimate path to joy and happiness. We must embrace self-compassion.

Living an authentic life in Christ is an everyday choice and must be viewed in that way. Like the alcoholic who gets up every day and says, "I will not have a drink today," we must have a one-day-at-a-time mentality.

There Is No Finish Line

Sooner or later the serious runner goes through a special, very personal experience that is unknown to most people.

Some call it euphoria. Others say it's a new kind of mystical experience that propels you into an elevated state of consciousness.

A flash of joy. A sense of floating as you run.

The experience is unique to each of us, but when it happens you break through a barrier that separates you from casual runners. Forever.

And from that point on, there is no finish line. You run for your life. You begin to be addicted to what running gives you.

We at Nike understand that feeling. There is no finish line for us either. We will never stop trying to excel, to produce running shoes that are better and better every year.

Beating the competition is relatively easy.

But beating yourself is a never-ending commitment.
—*Nike* [39]

When I was in high school, Nike came out with the tagline "There is no finish line" for a major ad campaign to support its line of running shoes. At the time, I was wrestling and had taken up competitive long-distance running. I was captivated by the message and the subsequent imagery of a lone runner journeying down a long and winding road. The words that described the scenario further captured my imagination and seemed to embody my personality and the spirit of work and dedication that leads to a life of success. I purchased the Nike poster and hung it on my wall as a symbol of life as a long and winding journey of consistency and daily commitment to my dream.

I kept that poster on my wall all through high school and college. "There is no finish line" became my personal tagline. It was a constant reminder that success comes to those who are willing to put in the daily work and effort to reach their goals. And even better, I learned that when you embrace the journey rather than the end result, the process can become richer and more impactful, enjoyable, and rewarding than the goal itself.

This certainly became part of my life's vision. Long after I stopped running competitively and wrestling, I have continued to exercise most days of my life. It is part of who I am and it is my daily victory over myself. It is an opportunity for me to exercise my will over my body every day.

This mentality has spilled into many other areas of my life as well. Whether the daily commitment is to my faith, family, or the world, I see it all in a very similar way. There is no finish line. Each day is a new opportunity to be successful, self-disciplined, and accountable to something greater than my own selfish needs.

I have also discovered that humans need to set themselves up for success. We need a plan that allows us to be successful even in the dynamic and ever-changing nature of life. I have come to realize that most people struggle in their faith life, not because of a lack of faith, but because of a lack of discipline and sense of long perspective.

When I look back in honesty on the ebb and flow of my own faith journey, I see the failures were much more a function of the process than anything else. I allowed the "rest of my life" to interfere with my commitment to my faith life.

Whether it was the strains of work or young children, I did not have a solid process that would allow for me to be successful on a daily basis. Ultimately, I needed to figure out a better way, a better plan that would keep me consistent. I discovered that the same process I used in business could be successful in my spiritual life as well. As I conclude this book, I think the basic notion of Jesuit leadership is as good a way as any to sum up the essential realities of leadership that we must come to terms with in order to continue making a difference in the world each day.

These principles are equally effective for your family life, your civic commitments, your church involvement—basically for every area of your life.

> We're all leaders, and we're leading all the time. Whether we are doing it well or poorly, chances are we are affecting someone else.

> Leadership springs from within. It is about who I am as much as what I do. Therefore, we must know who we are at our core. Even when we stray off our path, we have the foundation of knowledge to eventually come back to our core.

> Catholic leadership is not an act. It is my life, my way of living in a manner that honors our essential purpose.

> I never complete the task of becoming a leader. It's an ongoing process of self-reflection and self-evaluation.

The Jesuits' insight on leadership drives at the core of what we must accept if we are to become God's vision for us. We cannot simply stop being our best because it is inconvenient, or excuse ourselves, saying we don't have a "leadership personality." God has given all of us the task of leading people in our lives. He has also given us the tools to enhance these skills. Yet authentic leadership is not possible without the elements of virtue. It is the molecular structure of the character that is demanded of leaders.

A Vocation of Hope, Happiness, and Legacy

Work is a good thing for man—a good thing for his humanity—because
through work man not only transforms nature, adapting it to his own
needs, but he also achieves fulfillment as a human being and indeed, in
a sense, becomes "more a human being."
—St. John Paul II (Laborem Exercens, Through Work)

Now more than ever, we need leaders who dare to live their faith
in every aspect of their lives, including their work. It is easy to be
a hard-nosed, apathetic, or self-absorbed leader who only values
profits or his or her own short-term success. It is also very easy to
be a leader who cares only about relationships and making peers
and subordinates comfortable and accountable to merely average
results.

The real challenge for us is to create an environment that can
inspire others to live with compassion, empathy, and inspiration.
It is characterized by investing ourselves and being willing to be
the first. In essence, it is through virtue and charisma that we
are worthy of being respected and followed. Therefore, we don't
have to fall back on a given title or some coercive form of formal
power to get people to listen, follow, and deliver results. Reverent power in leadership will always trump leadership based on a
short-term formal power base.

Preparation and Restraint

The secret to being a bore is to tell everything.
—Voltaire

One of the essential characteristics of leadership is having the
discipline to thoroughly prepare yourself for whatever chal-

lenge or job awaits. Great leaders don't just "wing it." Whether it is being a perpetual student of the vocation you have chosen, doing the prep work required for the big meeting, or practicing diligently to deliver a speech, confidence and success come from preparation.

However, another critical aspect of leadership is knowing the power of restraint. This means having the humility to curtail a desire to grandstand with your knowledge in order to impress your audience beyond the intended objective.

In my experience, I have found the latter to be one of the most challenging and uncommon characteristics of leaders. It takes a good deal of confidence and humility to restrain oneself from being verbose. As a parent and business leader, I have to admit that I have failed to do this more often than I care to remember. But the fact is that over-lecturing simply does not work in parenting, business, or faith! We are all masters at tuning each other out very quickly.

In the Catholic Church, I find brevity to be a rare commodity. Preparation is a hallmark of the priesthood and of many Catholic authors and speakers. Most are highly educated and have spent much of their adult lives learning their craft, but then they want to "prove" it, or they struggle to convey that hard-earned knowledge in a way that is relevant, entertaining, and digestible.

However, there are several individuals who I believe will stand out as champions of the New Evangelization of the twenty-first century precisely because of their ability to harness preparation and restraint. Bishop Robert Barron and Cardinal Timothy Dolan are two such individuals. Interestingly enough, both of these men have very strong ties to the Midwest. They are modern-day versions of the great American evangelist of the twentieth century, Fulton Sheen (who was also a midwesterner).

Part of the magnetism and effectiveness of these men is their ability to convey the beauty and genius of Catholicism in a way that truly resonates with the everyday life of a wide and varying population of Christians in the United States today. They are incredibly knowledgeable about the philosophy and theology of our faith, but they communicate with a plainspoken, humble, and honest charm that is accessible to the everyday Christian.

They converse with honesty and humility that never seeks to talk above or below their intended audience. They use humor, modern cultural references, personal anecdotes, familiar language, pragmatic examples, and modern modes of communication to reach their audience in unique ways. They also challenge the reader or listener to go deeper with his or her spiritual and intellectual growth, reaffirming the difficult but worthy journey of what it means to practice Catholicism. Bishop Barron has written some very dense and intellectually challenging material as well, but he does so purposely, knowing he is writing to a very linear and particular audience and not for mass consumption.

"Beige Catholicism"

Bishop Robert Barron uses the term "beige Catholicism" to describe a Catholic culture that is overly accommodating to the prevailing secular culture, bland and unsure of its position, and apologetic of Catholic moral teaching and the tradition of our faith. It is a premise in which the world sets the agenda for the Church, rather than the Church being a beacon for the world, based on the truth of our faith.

Maybe beige Catholicism is a function of the misinterpreted spirit of post–Vatican II, or the clerical abuse crisis of the past twenty years. Regardless of the reason, both Barron and Dolan preach and lead in a way that is always respectfully inclusive, but never beige. They have shown that we can be strong, confident, and bold, while also being universal and generous in our approach to the greater culture.

As I've shared in this book, for much of my business career beige Catholicism was the standard by which I measured myself. Perhaps now you will have discovered that this term summarizes your vocation as a parent or business leader. Certainly, it is a much easier path to travel for all of us, because it takes less thought, creativity, time, and risk.

As humans, we make mistakes, but the message of the Gospels transcends the fragile humanity of its caretakers. Therefore, we must not allow the mistakes of our lives or those of our Church leaders to discourage us from boldly living our faith. Jesus was never bland or beige, nor were any of the great saints. We must remember that we have been chosen, and the reality of the truth forces us to make a choice that will not always lead to comfort or cultural acceptance. However, the measure of courage will be our willingness to resist the path of beige Catholicism or "cafeteria Catholicism" (referring to those who pick and choose what teachings they want to believe).

We Change the World One Life at a Time

Love is willing the good of the other . . . and then doing something concrete about it. It's not an emotion; it's not an attitude. It's a movement of the will.
—*Bishop Robert Barron* [40]

I have covered a considerable amount of ground in this book. I hope there were some ideas, personal anecdotes, quotes, or excerpts from Catholic social doctrine that resonated with you or challenged you. My desire in writing this book was for you to take away at least one idea or inspiration that will propel you forward in your life's path toward deeper love and sanctity. If this has happened, then I have achieved my goal and am honored to have played a small part in the movement of the New Evangelization.

I hope you will join me on this journey of incorporating your vocation as a platform for proactively living out your faith in culture. Together, we have the power to change the world.

AFTERWORD

Majuro, Marshall Islands, July 11, 2017

Your name shall no more be called Jacob, but Israel,
because you have striven with God and
with men and have prevailed.
—Genesis 32:28

It has been almost fifteen years since Kaaren and I first traveled to this remote coral-based island in Micronesia. We have returned once again, this time not to adopt, but simply to celebrate. Today was our twenty-fifth wedding anniversary and fifteen years since the adoption of our daughter, Kathryn, from this unique atoll.

In gratitude for these events and so many other blessings throughout our lives, we attended Mass at the Cathedral of the Assumption in Majuro today. We celebrated the Eucharist together as a family and then received a blessing from the local parish priest, Father Raymond. It was a special day for our family, indeed!

In meditating upon our twenty-fifth anniversary and the significance of being here this week, I was again reminded of the wisdom and insight of God's revealed Word. The reading for today was from the book of Genesis, chapter 32, verses 24–31. It is the story of Isaac's second son, Jacob, and his peculiar but profound confrontation with an unknown assailant. As the story goes, Jacob encounters a man he doesn't know and proceeds to wrestle with him through the night. By daybreak, Jacob tires of the seemingly endless struggle, eventually reaching a truce. However, he requests a blessing from the man as a condition of this respite. The unknown man then asks Jacob his name. After hearing it, he pronounces Jacob's name to be changed to Israel, which means "he who wrestles with God." He then provides the requested blessing. The passage ends as follows: "Jacob called the name of the place Peniel, saying, 'For I have seen God face to face, and yet my life is preserved.'"

Jacob's new name would become the name of the future nation formed by the tribes of his twelve sons. As we know, the nation and its descendants would do their own wrestling with God over the course of the history of salvation.

What a prophetic message for me to ponder on this momentous occasion in my life. For I have wrestled with doing the will of God for much of my life as well. I have grappled with him through pride, avarice, twenty-five years of marriage, in sickness, health, infertility, adoption, fatherhood, and the true call of vocation. But today as we received our silver jubilee marriage blessing from Father Raymond, I could only feel the overwhelming gratitude and humility of the goodness of God and his plan for my life.

Today there was no wrestling with God, but only blessings from him. For this life Kaaren and I have hoped, for these children we have been on our knees to pray, for this marriage we have fought, wept, labored, and loved. So the struggle of Israel is a metaphor for my struggle and probably your struggle as well. Yet with the ever-abundant grace provided by the sacramental nature of our faith, Christian hope is always possible. And with hope there can be happiness as well.

Through these adversities and triumphs, we have methodically sown the seeds of a life we could have never dreamed of twenty-five years ago. As it turns out, the cross is the salvific antidote that brings about our happiness. Today I feel the abundant joy of God's love for my family and all his people.

ABOUT THE AUTHOR

John Abbate is an independent franchisee/owner-operator of McDonald's restaurants throughout the Central Valley of California, as well as a strategic adviser to the Dynamic Catholic Institute. He is also co-founder and president of Possibility Productions (www.possibilityproductions.org), a nonprofit apostolate in support of the mission of the New Evangelization.

John holds a BBA in Economics from the University of San Diego, an MBA from the University of Notre Dame's Mendoza School of Business and an MA in Catholic Theology from the Augustine Institute. This is his first book.

John can be reached by email at
john.abbate@dynamiccatholic.com

NOTES

1. Thomas Aquinas, *Summa Theologica*, trans. Fathers of the English Dominican Province (New York: Benziger Bros., 1947–48), Part 1, Question 22, Article 3.

2. St. John Paul II, *Fides et Ratio* (Libreria Editrice Vaticana, 1998), 23.

3. A quote from the movie about C. S. Lewis' life, *Shadowlands*, adapted by William Nicholson from his play and directed by Richard Attenborough.

4. Pope Francis, *Lumen Fidei* (Libreria Editrice Vaticana), 4.

5. Thomas Merton, *The Seven Storey Mountain: An Autobiography of Faith* (New York: Houghton Mifflin Harcourt, 1999), p. 186.

6. Pope Francis, "Address of Pope Francis to the Participants in the Pilgrimage of Families During the Year of Faith" (Libreria Editrice Vaticana, 2013).

7. Erin El Issa, "2016 American Household Credit Card Debt Study," Nerdwallet, https://www.nerdwallet.com/blog/average-credit-card-debt-household/.

8. Thomas Merton, *New Seeds of Contemplation* (New York: New Directions, 1962), p. 78.

9. Gallup, http://news.gallup.com/poll/166211/worldwide -median-household-income-000.aspx.

10. St. John Paul II, *Centesimus Annus* (Libreria Editrice Vaticana, 1991), 42.

11. Ibid.

12. Michael Novak, *The Spirit of Democratic Capitalism* (Lanham, MD: Madison Books, 1982).

13. Pope Benedict XVI, "Fighting Poverty to Build Peace: Message for Celebration of the World Day of Peace" (Libreria Editrice Vaticana, 2009).

14. The Philanthropy Roundtable, http://www.philanthropy roundtable.org/almanac/statistics/.

15. Michael Douglas, *Wall Street*, directed by Oliver Stone (Los Angeles: Twentieth Century Fox, 1987).

16. Pope John Paul II, *Evangelium Vitae* (Libreria Editrice Vaticana, 1995), 74.

17. Paulo Coelho, *The Pilgrimage* (New York: HarperSanFrancisco, 1995).

18. C. S. Lewis, *Mere Christianity* (New York: Macmillan, 1960), pp. 55–56.

19. John Paul II, *Gaudium et Spes*, 24.

20. Robert Barron, *Catholicism: A Journey to the Heart of the Faith* (New York: Image Books, 2011), p. 43.

21. Alasdair MacIntyre, *After Virtue* (London: Bloomsbury Publishing, 2013), p. 290.

22. Aquinas, *Summa Theologica*, Part II, Question 17, Article 1.

23. Josemaría Escrivá, *Friends of God* (New York: Scepter, 2002), 292 .

24. John Paul II, 15th World Youth Day Address, *Tor Vergata*, (2000).

25. *Life and Works of Abraham Lincoln*, Centenary Edition, ed. Marion Mills Miller, Litt. D. (Princeton), Vol. V, p. 166.

26. Thomas Merton, *The Seven Storey Mountain: An Autobiography of Faith* (New York: Houghton Mifflin Harcourt, 1999), p. 223.

27. Benedict XVI, *Caritas in Veritate* (Libreria Editrice Vaticana, 2009), 57.

28. Matthew Archbold, *Faith under Fire: Dramatic Stories of Christian Courage* (Cincinnati: Servant, 2016).

29. Pope John Paul II, *Salvifici Doloris* (Libreria Editrice Vaticana, 1984), 23.

30. Ibid., 26.

31. Bishop Robert Barron, "Parable of the Talents," November 19, 2017; https://www.wordonfire.org/resources/homily/parable-of-the-talents/818/.

32. Pope Francis, "Meeting with Young People," impromptu speech given at Santo Tomas University, Manila, Philippines, January 18, 2015.

33. Pope Francis, *Laudato Si* (Libreria Editrice Vaticana, 2015), 217.

34. Ibid., 190.

35. Pacific Institute of Public Policy, "Pacific's High Teen Pregnancy Rates," Gif Johnson, April 22, 2014; http://pacificpolicy.org/2014/04/pacifics-high-teen-pregnancy-rates/.

36. Romano Guardini, *Letters from Lake Como: Explorations on Technology and the Human Race* (Grand Rapids, Mich.: William B. Eerdman's, 1994).

37. Ibid.

38. Annual apparition to Mirjana quoted in June Klins, *I Have Come to Tell the World That God Exists: The Best of "The Spirit of Medjugorje,"* Volume 3 (self-published, 2011), p. 274.

39. Created by John Brown & Partners in 1977 for Nike advertising campaign.

40. "Bishop Barron on Faith, Hope, and Love," YouTube video, 7:59, posted by WordonFire.org, January 31, 2013, https://www.youtube.com/watch?v=PuyKsaj6GbM&feature=em-subs_digest.

NOTES

NOTES

NOTES

NOTES

NOTES

NOTES

HAVE YOU EVER WONDERED HOW THE CATHOLIC FAITH COULD HELP YOU LIVE BETTER?

How it could help you find more *joy* at work, *manage* your personal finances, *improve* your marriage, or make you a *better* parent?

THERE IS GENIUS IN CATHOLICISM.

When *Catholicism* is lived as it is intended to be, it elevates every part of our lives. It may sound simple, but they say *genius is taking something complex and making it simple.*

Dynamic Catholic started with a dream: to help ordinary people discover the *genius of Catholicism.*

Wherever you are in your journey, we want to meet you there and walk with you, *step by step*, helping you to discover God and become *the-best-version-of-yourself.*

To find more helpful resources, visit us online at DynamicCatholic.com.

◨ Dynamic Catholic

FEED YOUR SOUL.